Vicky
TOMOPOULAI

0123456789

Laurence King Publishing Ltd
361–373 City Road
London EC1V 1LR
United Kingdom
Tel: + 44 20 7841 6900
Fax: + 44 20 7841 6910
e-mail: enquiries@laurenceking.com
www.laurenceking.com

A catalogue record for this
book is available
from the British Library

ISBN: 978-1-78067-003-4

Design: Roger Fawcett-Tang,
Struktur Design

Printed in China

For Malcolm,
the king of numbers
DN 777

0123456789

Numbers in Graphic Design

Roger Fawcett-Tang

Laurence King Publishing

123
456
789

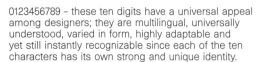

0123456789 – these ten digits have a universal appeal among designers; they are multilingual, universally understood, varied in form, highly adaptable and yet still instantly recognizable since each of the ten characters has its own strong and unique identity.

Numbers in Graphic Design focuses on how graphic designers tackle the ordering of number-heavy information, from timetables to annual reports and other data-rich documents through to highly creative and playful typographic experiments exploring the most abstract notion of numeric information.

The content is broken up into eight chapters that illustrate how hard working these digits are. *Addition* showcases a variety of timelines both within exhibition graphics and on the printed page, and how a timeframe can help to organize variable data such as illustrations, objects, interactive media and the written word. *Data* looks at a wide variety of information graphics. While numbers are not always the 'hero' of design, they do form the foundations and structure of all the illustrated design systems. *Order* features timetables for bus, train and tram networks plus a wide variety of events listings and schedules, highlighting both the day-to-day practicals of clear tabulated typography and the more expressive solutions. *Chronology* focuses on time: from calendars and diaries to watches and various screen-based solutions to charting and expressing the passage of seconds, minutes and hours. *Abstraction* reveals a variety of creative directions in which numerals can be expressed, and how far the typographic forms can be pushed while still mantaining the essence of the character. Vernacular typographic solutions show numeric forms found in the everyday. *Form* is all about when the design focuses on the number or a sequence of numbers within a range of contexts, from the formal to the decorative. *Multiplication* navigates its way around signage and wayfinding systems within architecture, and also illustrates super-sized numbers on the printed page, adding a sense of epic scale to both structure and content. Finally, *Subtraction* looks at how far the number can be simplified while mantaining legibility – doing much more with far less.

When recently asked me what my favourite number was, I replied 'it depends on the font; I love all ten of them.' Numbers have a great power to convey highly detailed information in a clear and logical manner – be it complex timetables or annual reports. They can also help navigate you around a building or the pages of a book.

Helvetica
50 —

1957 — 07 —
1,576,800,000 s
26,280,000 mins
438,000 hrs
18250 days

01.
Addition

Timelines

Counting methods

50 image makers
s 50x50 cm
Edition of 50

01.1.1
Timelines:
Three-dimensional realization

A three-dimensional timeline extends
the length of the gallery for an
exhibition on the history of Formula
One racing. Each decade is marked
out in huge lettering on the floor with
the relevant cars positioned according
to their place along the timeline. The
wall contains information panels and
artefacts such as race programmes
and tickets from historical Formula
One events.

01
Studio Myerscough
Formula One
Design Museum, London
Touring exhibition

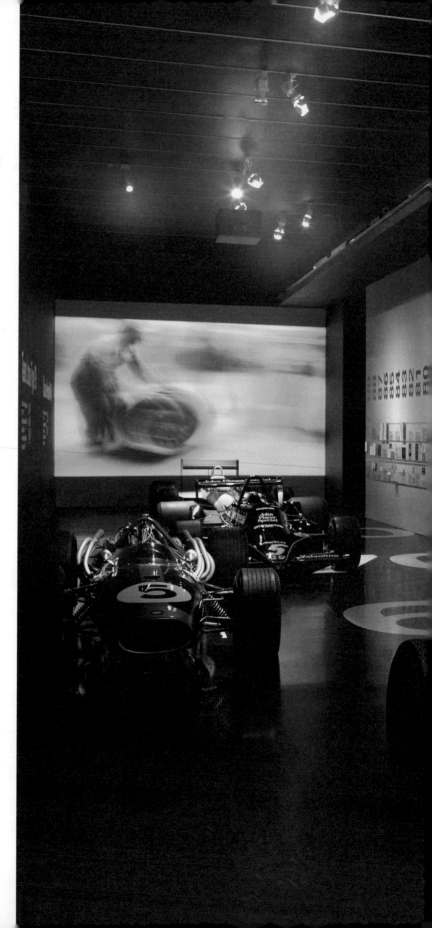

01.1.1
Timelines:
Three-dimensional realization

In a move away from the conventional use of adhesive vinyl lettering applied to the gallery wall, the *Super Contemporary* exhibition uses three wooden rails to form the structure of the timeline. A groove in the edge of each rail allows information cards, images and artefacts to be propped up along the length of the timeline. The top rail includes larger black information panels with thematic titles together with smaller red year markers. In a break from the usual, purely linear nature of a timeline, larger items of furniture are accommodated into the line as the wooden rail extends down to ground level with larger wooden platforms.

02
Bibliothèque
Super Contemporary
Design Museum, London

David Adjaye
Ron Arad
BarberOsgerby
Neville Brody
Nigel Coates
Paul Cocksedge
Tom Dixon
El Ultimo Grito
with Urban Salon
Kit Grover
Zaha Hadid
Thomas Heatherwick
Wayne Hemingway
Industrial Facility
Ross Phillips
Paul Smith

Design Museum
Shad Thames
London SE1 2YD
Designmuseum.org

Design Museum and
Beefeater 24
invite you to celebrate
the opening of
Super Contemporary
7–9pm
2 June 2009

RSVP essential
rsvp@designmuseum.org
Admits two
Non transferable

Design Museum
and Beefeater 24 present
Super
Contemporary

BEEFEATER 24

DESIGN
MUSEUM

01.1.2
Timelines:
Interaction

For *WerkStadt Dialog*, conventional
exhibition timeline panels are
combined with an interactive screen-
based element. The screen runs
along the length of the glass-covered
information panels and triggers video-
based sequences as it moves over
the appropriate part of the display.
The screen-based interface mirrors
the design and layout of the static
display graphics.

01
L2M3 Kommunikationsdesign
WerkStadt Dialog
Mercedes-Benz, Daimler AG

01.1.3
Timelines:
Windows

The grid formed by the white exhibition panels in *Great Moments of a Patron* helps organize the different levels of information printed on the surface. An understated monochromatic look is achieved through the use of light weight sans serif typography, which is complemented by the inclusion of the signatures of key historical figures printed in a pale grey.

The minimal design of the exhibition is enlivened by the inclusion of 'windows' that feature various written artefacts. The protruding frames of these display boxes feature black-and-white portraits of the historical figures. As the portraits are printed on the sides of the frames, they are visible only when the exhibition is viewed from an angle and do not distract when visitors look directly at the display windows.

01
L2M3 Kommunikationsdesign
Great Moments of a Patron
Staatsbibliothek, Berlin

1839
Louis Daguerre schreibt vom Export seiner Erfindung nach England.
→ S. 108

1839
Charles Darwin schickt Alexander von Humboldt Ergebnisse von Temperaturmessungen im Pazifik.
→ S. 110

1841
Emil Du Bois-Reymond zeichnet eine Versuchsanordnung zum Messen des Froschstroms.
→ S. 112

Vor 100 Jahren schenkte Ludwig Darmstaedter der Königlichen Bibliothek seine Autographensammlung. Die Staatsbibliothek zu Berlin ehrt ihren großen Mäzen mit dieser Ausstellung.

60 Dokumente der berühmtesten Persönlichkeiten aus Wissenschaft, Kunst, Literatur und Geschichte sind Beispiele für die Universalität der über 250.000 Dokumente umfassenden Sammlung.

01.1.4
Timelines:
Expressive lines

The *K2 Sporting Moments 2010* series
of limited edition prints was created
for a management training company
to accompany a course of seminars
based on the concept of the 'athlete at
work'. Each print takes key elements
of data from a classic sporting event
and transforms the raw information
into a graphic timeline of the event,
taking into account speed, distance,
time, etc. The winner is depicted
in gold and the other competitors
are printed in grey. In each case
the abstracted graph illustrates the
essence of the event: two concentric
circles represent the athletes running
two laps of the track during the course
of the 800m race; wavy lines convey
the flow of water around a swimmer's
body, and so on.

Dame Kelly Holmes   Women's 800m, Athens   Women's 1,500m, Athens

01

01
Accept and Proceed
K2 Sporting Moments 2010
Dame Kelly Holmes,
Women's 800m race,
Athens Olympics, 2004

02
Accept and Proceed
K2 Sporting Moments 2008
James Cracknell, Steve
Redgrave, Tim Foster and
Matthew Pinsent taking the
Men's Coxless Fours gold
medal, Sydney Olympics, 2000

03, 04
Accept and Proceed
K2 Sporting Moments 2010
Mark Foster and
Alexander Popov,
Men's 50m freestyle,
Barcelona World
Championships, 2003

02

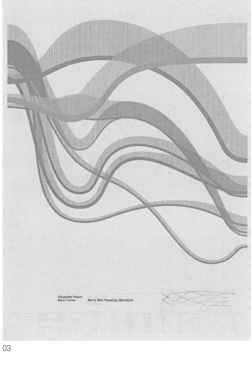

03

04

01.1.5
Timelines:
Strokes and lines

These two prints from the 'athlete at work' series (see page 18) feature day 4 of the US Open in San Diego, 2004, with Tiger Woods against Rocco Mediate. The circular graphic reflects the strokes played by each golfer during that day's play. The second print illustrates Lewis Hamilton's first victory at the Montreal Grand Prix, 2007. This graphic reflects the shifting positions taken by each driver thoughout the duration of the race.

01, 02
Accept and Proceed
K2 Sporting Moments 2008
Tiger Woods,
US Open, 2008

03
Accept and Proceed
K2 Sporting Moments 2008
Lewis Hamilton,
Montreal Grand Prix, 2007

01

02

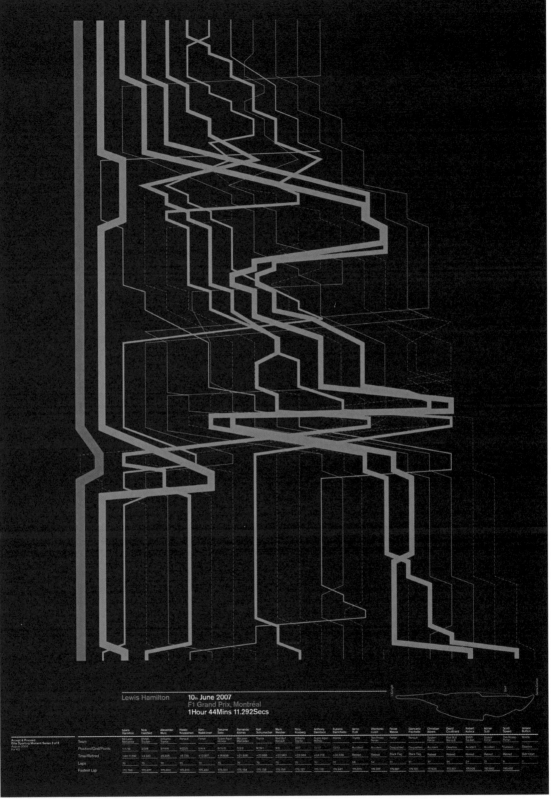

01.1.6
Timelines:
Concentric rhythms

This print from the 'athlete at work' series (see pages 18–21) illustrates Paula Radcliffe's victory at the 2005 London Marathon. The overlapping concentric circles reflect the rhythm and pace during the 26-mile journey around the heart of London.

01
Accept and Proceed
K2 Sporting Moments 2008
Paula Radcliffe,
London Marathon, 2005

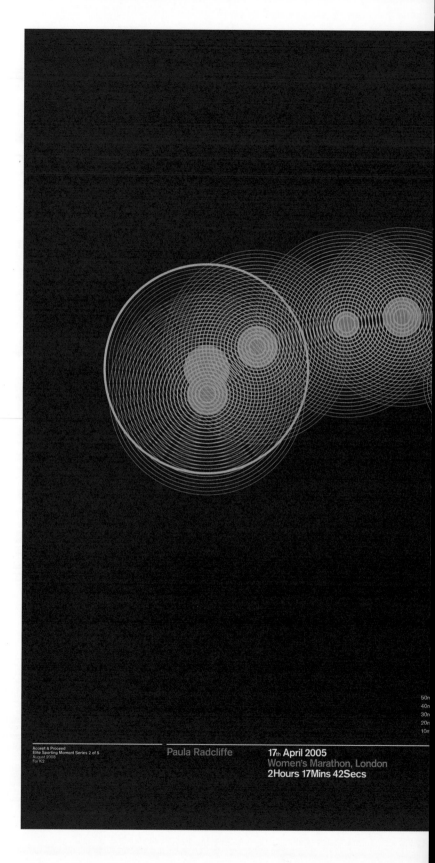

Accept & Proceed
Elite Sporting Moment Series 2 of 5
August 2008
For K2

Paula Radcliffe

17th **April 2005**
Women's Marathon, London
2Hours 17Mins 42Secs

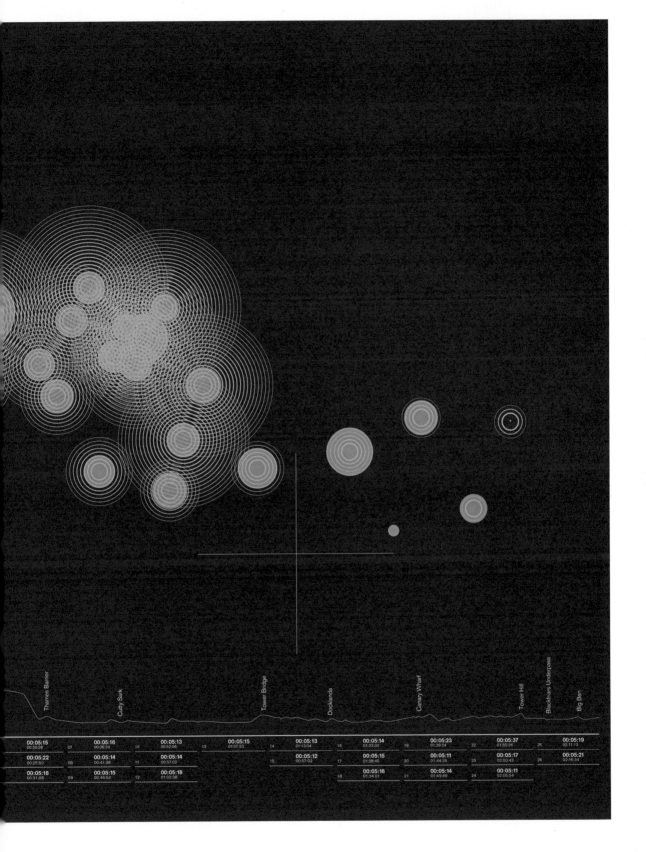

Thames Barrier

Cutty Sark

Tower Bridge

Docklands

Canary Wharf

Tower Hill

Blackfriars Underpass

Big Ben

00:05:15 00:20:28		00:05:16 00:36:24		00:05:13 00:52:06		00:05:15 01:07:53	14	00:05:13 01:13:04	16	00:05:14 01:23:30	19	00:05:23 01:39:24	22	00:05:37 01:55:26	25	00:05:19 02:11:13
00:05:22 00:25:50	07	00:05:14 00:41:38	10	00:05:14 00:57:02	13		15	00:05:12 00:57:02	17	00:05:15 01:28:45	20	00:05:11 01:44:35	23	00:05:17 02:00:43	26	00:05:21 02:16:34
00:05:18 00:31:08	08	00:05:15 00:46:53	11	00:05:18 01:02:38	12			00:05:16 01:34:01	18	00:05:14 01:49:49	21	00:05:11 02:05:54	24			

A set of two posters – *Hours of Dark 2007* and *Hours of Light 2007* – charts the daylight hours in London during the course of 2007. The dataline is shown as a series of concentric circles for the hours of light and horizontal lines for the hours of darkness. All the data for the year is listed at the foot of each poster, printed in a phosphorescent ink.

01, 02
Accept and Proceed
Hours of Dark 2007
A1 Screen print

03
Accept and Proceed
Hours of Light 2007
A1 Screen print

01

02

Hours of light 2007

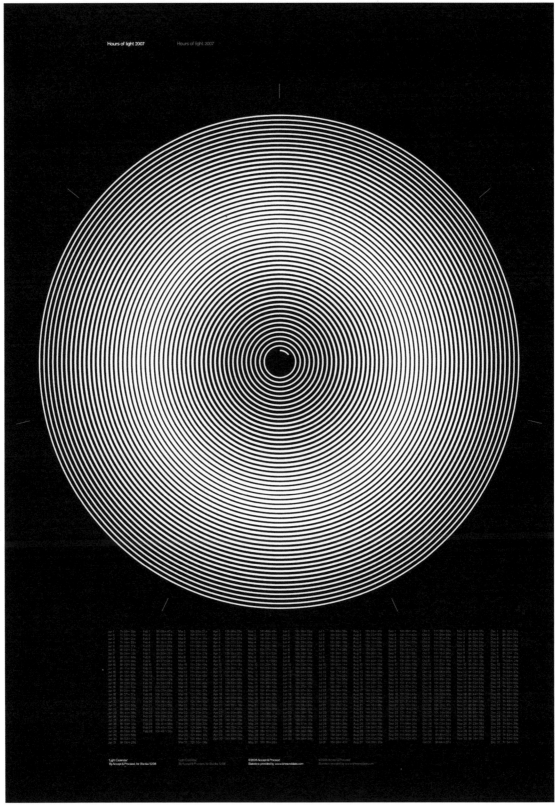

01.1.8
Timelines:
Graphic arcs

Accept and Proceed's *Hours of Light 2008* continues the series of light and dark posters (see pages 24–25).

Image Now's A1 poster illustrates a timeline of the historic battle between the two boxing legions Muhammad Ali and George Foreman in 1974. Each arc represents a round, with markers illustrating the punches.

01
Accept and Proceed
Hours of Light 2008
A1 Screen print

02
Image Now
*Muhammad Ali
v George Foreman*
Kinshasa, Zaire,
30 October 1974

01

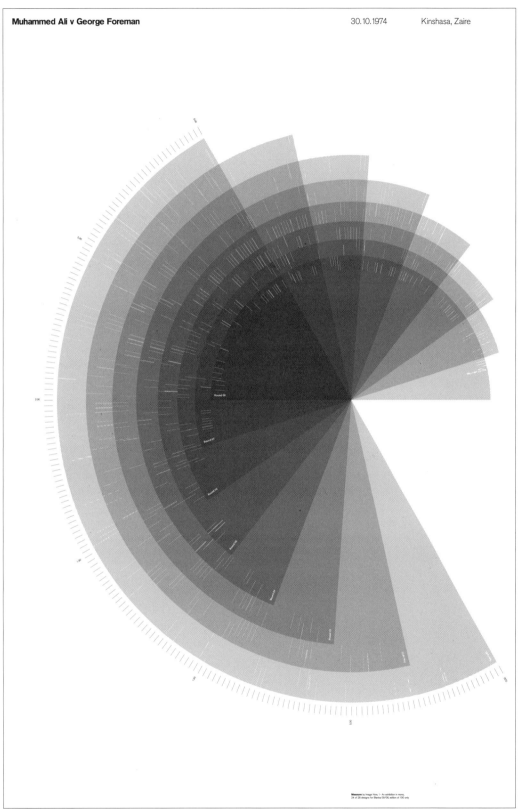

01.1.9
Timelines:
Spidergraph

Starting with his first book design in 1998, this timeline by Joost Grootens shows the expanding sequence of book designs he produced over a ten-year period. Small icons numbered from 1 to 100 identify the books and appear throughout *I swear I use no art at all* to indicate which book is being referred to. A simple date line runs across the foot of the spread and all the book information ranges off these positions. A series of connecting lines shows how one project led to another and the relationship between different projects over the time period.

01
Joost Grootens
I swear I use no art at all
Hairline rules are used to illustrate the connections from project to project.

Beginnings
This overview shows how one project led to another. Encounters or collaborations that resulted in new projects. It shows how non-book projects evolved into book projects.

Public s
De Mat
Justus
Raoul B
Baukje

Internship:
Raoul Bunschoten

Final project:
Public space project:
'Monument voor de meisje
van de balletacademie',

Education:
Gerrit Rietveld Academy,
Amsterdam
Architectural Design
Frans Bevers

Final project:
Interactive animation:
HOUSE

External examiners:
Winy Maas
Jacob van Rijs

Study project:
Braille Doorhandle

Interactive anima
exhibition 'Rotte
NAI, Rotterdam
MVRDV
Winy Maas
Jacob van Rijs
Nathalie de Vries

Cd-rom
Parkst
Stichti
Esther
Bindel

| 1990 | 1994 | 1995 | 1996 |

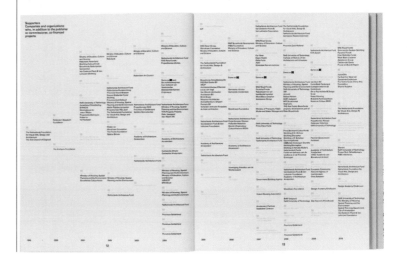

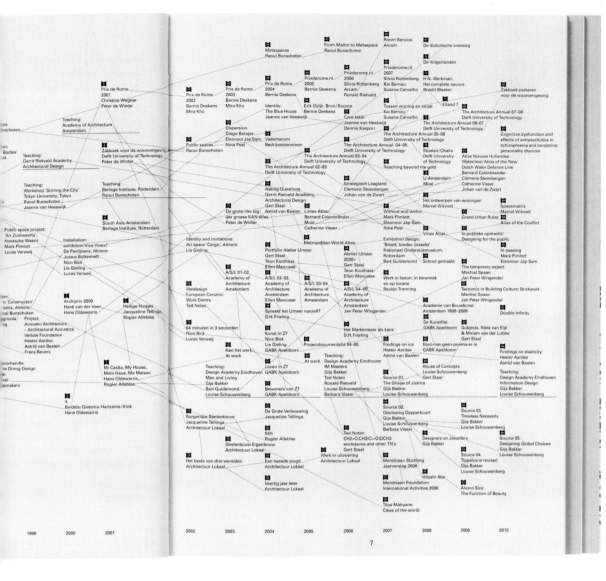

Metaspaces
Raoul Bunschoten

From Matter to Metaspace
Raoul Bunschoten

Room Service
Arcam

De diabolische snelweg

De Volgerlanden

Prix de Rome
2001
Christine Wagner
Peter de Winter

Prix de Rome
2002
Bernie Deekens
Mira Kho

Prix de Rome
2003
Bernie Deekens
Mira Kho

Prix de Rome
2004
Bernie Deekens

Prixderome.nl
2005
Bernie Deekens

Prixderome.nl
2006
Silvia Rottenberg
Arcam
Ronald Rietveld

Prixderome.nl
2007
Silvia Rottenberg
Kai Bernau
Susana Carvalho

H.N. Werkman.
Het complete oeuvre
Brecht Bleeker

Zakboek parkeren
voor de woonomgeving

Teaching:
Academy of Architecture
Amsterdam

Identity:
The Blue House
Jeanne van Heeswijk

Erik Odijk. Bron/Source
Bernie Deekens

Tussen woning en straat
Kai Bernau
Susana Carvalho

Erland 7

The Architecture Annual 07–08
Delft University of Technology

Zakboek voor de woonomgeving
Delft University of Technology
Peter de Winter

Dispersion
Diego Barajas
Eleonoor Jap Sam
Nina Post

Care-taker
Jeanne van Heeswijk
Dennis Kaspori

The Architecture Annual 06–07
Delft University of Technology

Cognitive dysfunction and
effects of antipsychotics in
schizophrenia and borderline
personality disorder

Teaching:
Gerrit Rietveld Academy,
Architectural Design

Public spaces
Raoul Bunschoten

Vademecum
Bedrijventerreinen

The Architecture Annual 05–06
Delft University of Technology

The Architecture Annual 04–05
Delft University of Technology

Stoelen/Chairs
Delft University
of Technology

Atlas Nieuwe Hollandse
Waterlinie/Atlas of the New
Dutch Water Defence Line
Bernard Colenbrander

Teaching:
Workshop 'Stirring the City'
Tokyo University, Tokyo
Raoul Bunschoten
Jeanne van Heeswijk

Teaching:
Berlage Institute, Rotterdam
Raoul Bunschoten

The Architecture Annual 03–04
Delft University of Technology

The Architecture Annual 02–03
Delft University of Technology

Reaching beyond the gold

Strategisch Laagland
Clemens Steenbergen
Johan van de Zwart

IJ Amsterdam
Must

Clemens Steenbergen
Catherine Visser
Johan van de Zwart

Asking Questions
Gerrit Rietveld Academy,
Architectural Design

De grote/the big/
der grosse KAN atlas
Peter de Winter

Limes Atlas/
Astrid van Baalen

Limes Atlas/
Bernard Colenbrander
Must
Catherine Visser

Without and within
Mark Pimlott
Eleonoor Jap Sam
Nina Post

Het ontwerpen van woningen
Marcel Witvoet

Spacematrix
Marcel Witvoet

South Axis Amsterdam
Berlage Institute, Rotterdam

Grand Urban Rules

Atlas of the Conflict

Public space project:
'Air Zuidwaarts',
Hoeksche Waard
Mark Pimlott
Lucas Verweij

Installation:
exhibition'Viva Vinex!'
De Paviljoens, Almere
Justus Bottenheft
Nico Bick
Lia Gieling
Lucas Verweij

Identity and invitations:
Art space 'Cargo', Almere
Lia Gieling

Metropolitan World Atlas

Portfolio Atelier IJmeer
Gert Staal
Teun Kooihaas
Ellen Marcusse

Atelier IJmeer
2030+
Gert Staal
Teun Kooihaas
Ellen Marcusse

Exhibition design:
'Breed, breder, breedst'
Nationaal Onderwijsmuseum,
Rotterdam
Bart Guldemond

School gemaakt

In publieke opdracht/
Designing for the public

In passing
Mark Pimlott
Eleonoor Jap Sam

Weldesign
European Ceramic
Work Centre
Ted Noten

A/S/L 01–02
Academy of
Architecture
Amsterdam

A/S/L 02–03
Academy of
Architecture
Amsterdam
Ellen Marcusse

A/S/L 03–04
Academy of
Architecture
Amsterdam

A/S/L 04–05
Academy of
Architecture
Amsterdam
Jan Peter Wingender

Werk in beton, in keramiek
en op locatie
Baukje Trenning

The temporary expert
Machiel Spaan
Jan Peter Wingender

Tectonics in Building Culture: Brickwork
Machiel Spaan
Jan Peter Wingender

Archiprix 2000
Henk van der Veen
Hans Oldewarris

Heilige Huisjes
Jacqueline Tellinga
Rogier Alleblas

Spreekt het IJmeer vanzelf?
D.H. Frieling

Het Markermeer als kans
D.H. Frieling

Academie van Bouwkunst
Amsterdam 1908–2008

Double Infinity

64 minuten in 3 seconden
Nico Bick
Lucas Verweij

Kunst in Z?
Nico Bick
Lia Gieling
GABK Apeldoorn

Projectdocumentatie 04–05

Findings on ice
Hester Aardse
Astrid van Baalen

De Kunstflat
GABK Apeldoorn

Kooi-met-geen-poema-er-in
GABK Apeldoorn

Subjects. Niels van Eijk
& Miriam van der Lubbe
Gert Staal

Findings on elasticity
Hester Aardse
Astrid van Baalen

Aan het werk/
At work

Teaching:
Design Academy Eindhoven
Man and Living
Gijs Bakker
Bart Guldemond
Louise Schouwenberg

Leven in Z?
GABK Apeldoorn

Bewoners van Z?
GABK Apeldoorn

Teaching:
Design Academy Eindhoven
IM Masters
Gijs Bakker
Ted Noten
Ronald Rietveld
Louise Schouwenberg
Barbara Visser

House of Concepts
Louise Schouwenberg
Gert Staal

Source 01.
The Shape of Justice
Gijs Bakker
Louise Schouwenberg

Teaching:
Design Academy Eindhoven
Information Design
Gijs Bakker
Louise Schouwenberg

Mi Casita, My House,
Mein Haus, Ma Maison
Hans Oldewarris,
Rogier Alleblas

4.
Bindels/Gietema/Hartzema/Klok
Hans Oldewarris

Burgerlijke Stedenbouw
Jacqueline Tellinga
Architectuur Lokaal

De Grote Verbouwing
Jacqueline Tellinga

Source 02.
Disclosing Dapperbuurt
Gijs Bakker
Louise Schouwenberg
Barbara Visser

Source 03.
Timeless Necessity
Gijs Bakker
Louise Schouwenberg

Stedenbouw Eigenbouw
Architectuur Lokaal

Still
Rogier Alleblas
Architectuur Lokaal

Ted Noten.
CH2=C(CH3)C(=O)OCH3
enclosures and other TN's
Gert Staal

Designers on Jewellery
Gijs Bakker

Source 05.
Designing Global Choices
Gijs Bakker
Louise Schouwenberg

Het beste van drie werelden
Architectuur Lokaal

Een tweede jeugd
Architectuur Lokaal

Werk in uitvoering
Architectuur Lokaal

Mondriaan Stichting
Jaarverslag 2006

Source 04.
Tippelzone revised
Gijs Bakker
Louise Schouwenberg

Veertig jaar later
Architectuur Lokaal

Hitoshi Abe
Mondriaan Foundation
International Activities 2006

Alvaro Siza:
The Function of Beauty

Titus Matiyane.
Cities of the world

1999   2000   2001   2002   2003   2004   2005   2006   2007   2008   2009   2010

01.1.10
Timelines:
Linear

This 432-page history of Daimler AG
comprises three chronicles in one:
detailed biographies of Karl Friedrich
Benz, Gottlieb Daimler and Wilhelm
Maybach, a chronology of Daimler
AG from 1883 to 2011 and 20 car
stories, each relating one topic from
the history of the company, brand
and product – visually and in terms of
content. A silver ribbon runs through
the book which acts as both timeline
and information bar containing caption
details and related notes.

01
L2M3 Kommunikationsdesign
Daimler Chronik
125 years of car history

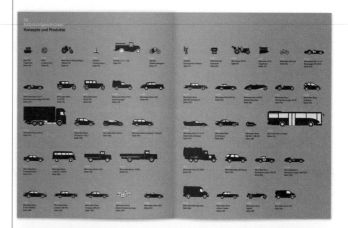

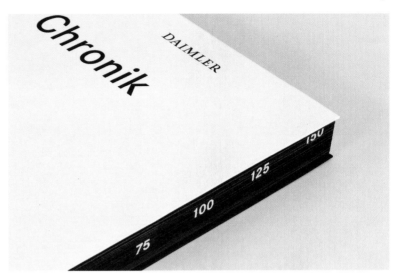

Chronik

DAIMLER

150 125 100 75

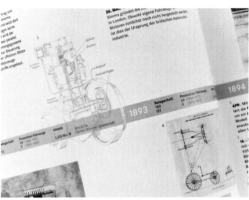

Frozen Dreams, a book on contemporary Russian art, adopts a space-efficient method for a two-page timeline of events in the Russian art world from 1963 to the present. The density of information varies from year to year, so to conserve space only the years with events are listed. This method, although compact, loses the sense of time and the pace of events.

Unleashed, a book on contemporary Turkish art, is part of the same series as *Frozen Dreams*. Its timeline is set over four pages, which means a more conventional horizontal method can be used. Each decade runs across the pages, allowing a clear understanding of the density of information from year to year.

The Sites of Ancient Greece features an extensive multilayered timeline which extends over 12 pages, starting at 3000 BC and continuing until AD 1900. With such a vast period to cover, and the variable levels of information held within it, the timeline uses a flexible system that depends on the volume of information within each period. As can be seen, 3000 to 2000 BC occupies the same space as 480 to 460 BC. The information is split into three horizontal bands: historical events, archaeological sites, and art and cultural events.

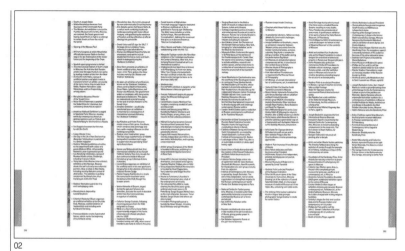

02

02
Struktur Design
Frozen Dreams:
Contemporary Art from Russia
Historical art timeline

03
Struktur Design
Unleashed:
Contemporary Art from Turkey
Historical art timeline

04
Struktur Design
The Sites of Ancient Greece
By Georg Gerster
Historical timeline of ancient
Greece

03

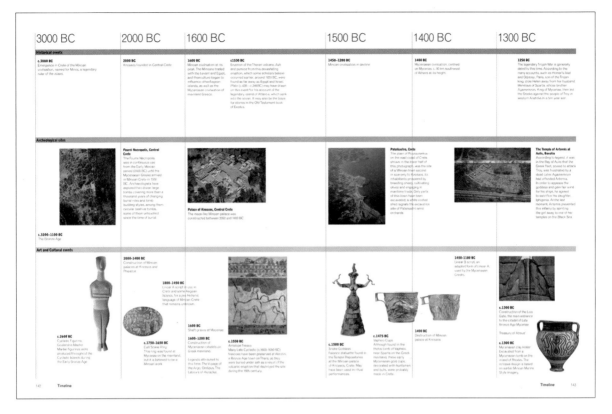

3000 BC | 2000 BC | 1600 BC | 1500 BC | 1400 BC | 1300 BC

Historical events

c.3000 BC Emergence in Crete of the Minoan civilisation, named for Minos, a legendary ruler of the island.

2000 BC Knossos founded in Central Crete.

1600 BC Minoan civilisation at its peak. The Minoans traded with the Levant and Egypt, and their culture began to influence other Aegean islands, as well as the Mycenaean civilisation of mainland Greece.

c.1530 BC Eruption of the Theran volcano. Ash and pumice from the devastating eruption, which some scholars believe occurred earlier, around 1650 BC, were found as far away as Egypt and Israel. Plato (c.428–c.348BC) may have drawn on this event for his account of the legendary island of Atlantis, which sank into the ocean. It may also be the basis for stories in the Old Testament book of Exodus.

1450–1200 BC Minoan civilisation in decline.

1400 BC Mycenaean civilisation, centred on Mycenae, c.90 km southwest of Athens at its height.

1250 BC The legendary Trojan War is generally dated to this time. According to the many accounts, such as Homer's Iliad and Odyssey, Paris, son of the Trojan king, stole Helen away from her husband Menelaus of Sparta, whose brother Agamemnon, king of Mycenae, then led the Greeks against the people of Troy in western Anatolia in a ten-year war.

Archaeological sites

Fourni Necropolis, Central Crete The Fourni Necropolis was in continuous use from the Early Minoan period (3500 BC) until the Mycenaean-Greeks arrived in Minoan Crete in 1500 BC. Archaeologists have explored two dozen large tombs covering more than a thousand years of changing burial rites and tomb building styles, among them circular beehive tombs, some of them untouched since the time of burial.

c.3200–1100 BC The Bronze Age

Palace of Knossos, Central Crete The maze-like Minoan palace was constructed between 2000 and 1400 BC.

Palaikastro, Crete The town of Palaeokastro on the east coast of Crete shown in this photograph, was the site of a Minoan town second in size only to Knossos. Its inhabitants prospered by breeding sheep, cultivating olives and engaging in maritime trade. Only parts of this town have been excavated; a white-roofed shed signals the excavation site of Palaikastro and orchards.

The Temple of Artemis at Aulis, Boeotia According to legend, it was in the bay of Aulis that the Greek fleet, poised to attack Troy, was frustrated by a dead calm. Agamemnon had offended Artemis. In order to appease the goddess and gain fair wind for his ships, he agreed to sacrifice his daughter, Iphigenia. At the last moment, Artemis prevented this dismay by spiriting the girl away to one of her temples on the Black Sea.

Art and Cultural events

c.2600 BC Cycladic Figurines Goulandris Master Marble figurines were produced throughout the Cycladic Islands during the Early Bronze Age.

2000–1400 BC Construction of Minoan palaces at Knossos and Phaistos.

1800–1450 BC Linear A script in use in Crete and some Aegean Islands, for a pre-Hellenic language of Minoan Crete that remains unknown.

c.1750–1650 BC Gold Screw Ring This ring was found at Mycenae on the mainland, but it is believed to be a Minoan work.

1600 BC Shaft graves at Mycenae.

1600–1200 BC Construction of Mycenaean citadels on Greek mainland.

c.1550 BC Antelope Fresco Many Late Cycladic (c.1600–1050 BC) frescoes have been preserved at Akrotiri, a Bronze Age town on Thera, as they were buried under ash as a result of the volcanic eruption that destroyed the site during the 16th century.

c.1500 BC Snake Goddess Faience statuette found in the Temple Repositories at the Minoan palace of Knossos, Crete. May have been used in ritual performances.

c.1475 BC Vaphrio Cups Although found in the tholos tomb of Vaphrio, near Sparta on the Greek mainland, these early Mycenaean gold cups, decorated with huntsmen and bulls, were probably made in Crete.

1400 BC Destruction of Minoan palace at Knossos.

1450–1180 BC Linear B script, an adapted form of Linear A, used by the Mycenaean Greeks.

c.1300 BC Construction of the Lion Gate, the main entrance to the citadel of Late Bronze Age Mycenae. Treasury of Atreus!

c.1300 BC Mycenaean clay Krater Excavated from a Mycenaean tomb on the island of Rhodes. The octopus design is based on earlier Minoan Marine Style imagery.

142 Timeline

143 Timeline

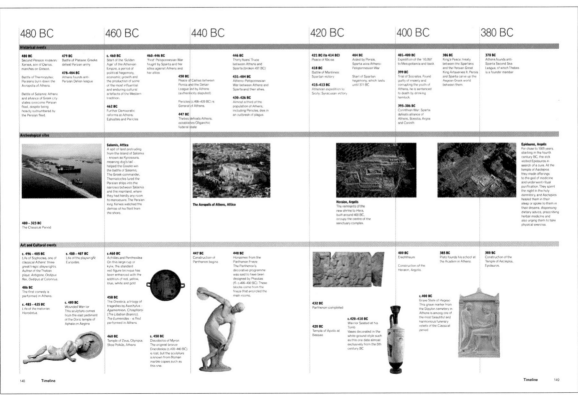

480 BC | 460 BC | 440 BC | 420 BC | 400 BC | 380 BC

Historical events

480 BC Second Persian invasion: Xerxes, son of Darius, marches on Greece. Battle of Thermopylae: Persians burn down the Acropolis of Athens. Battle of Salamis: Athens and alliance of Greek city states overcome Persian fleet, despite being heavily outnumbered by the Persian fleet.

479 BC Battle of Plataea: Greeks defeat Persian army.

478–404 BC Athens founds anti-Persian Delian league.

c. 460 BC Start of the 'Golden Age' of the Athenian Empire, a period of political hegemony, economic growth and the production of some of the most influential and enduring cultural artefacts of the Western tradition.

462 BC Further Democratic reforms at Athens. Ephialtes and Pericles.

460–446 BC 'First' Peloponnesian War fought by Sparta and her allies against Athens and her allies.

458 BC Peace of Callias between Persia and the Delian League (but its authenticity disputed). Pericles (c.495–429 BC) is General of Athens.

447 BC Thebes defeats Athens, establishes Oligarchic federal state.

446 BC Thirty Years' Truce between Athens and Sparta (broken 431 BC).

421 BC (to 414 BC) Peace of Nicias.

418 BC Battle of Mantinea: Spartan victory.

431–404 BC Athenian-Peloponnesian War between Athens and Sparta and their allies.

430–426 BC Almost a third of the population of Athens, including Pericles, dies in an outbreak of plague.

404 BC Aided by Persia, Sparta wins Atheno-Peloponnesian War. Start of Spartan hegemony, which lasts until 371 BC.

401–400 BC Expedition of the '10,000' to Mesopotamia and back.

399 BC Trial of Socrates. Found guilty of impiety and corrupting the youth of Athens, he is sentenced to death by drinking hemlock.

395–386 BC Corinthian War: Sparta defeats alliance of Athens, Boeotia, Argos and Corinth.

386 BC King's Peace: treaty between the Spartans and the Persian Great King Artaxerxes II. Persia carve up the Aegean Greek world between them.

378 BC Athens founds anti-Spartan Second Sea League, of which Thebes is a founder member.

Archaeological sites

Salamis, Attica A spit of land protruding from the island of Salamis – known as Kynosoura, meaning dog's tail – helped the Greeks win the battle of Salamis. The Greek commander, Themistocles lured the Persian ships into the narrows between Salamis and the mainland, where they had hardly any room to manoeuvre. The Persian king Xerxes watched the demise of his fleet from the shore.

480 – 323 BC The Classical Period

The Acropolis of Athens, Attica

Heraion, Argolis The remnants of the new shrine to Hera, built around 400 BC, occupy the centre of the sanctuary complex.

Epidauros, Argolis For close to 1000 years, starting in the fourth century BC, the sick visited Epidauros in search of a cure. At the sanctuary of Asclepius they made offerings to the god of medicine and underwent ritual purification. They spent the night in the holy dormitory, and Asclepius helped them in their sleep or spoke to them in their dreams, dispensing dietary advice, prescribing herbal medicine and also urging them to take physical exercise.

Art and Cultural events

c. 496 – 405 BC Life of Sophocles, one of classical Athens' three great tragic playwrights. Author of the Theban plays: Antigone, Oedipus Rex, Oedipus at Colonus.

486 BC The first comedy is performed in Athens.

c. 485 – 425 BC Life of the historian Herodotus.

c. 480 – 407 BC Life of the playwright Euripides.

c. 480 BC Wounded Warrior This sculpture comes from the east pediment of the Doric temple of Aphaia on Aegina.

c.460 BC Achilles and Penthesilea On this large cup or kylix, the standard red-figure technique has been enhanced with the addition of red, yellow, blue, white and gold.

458 BC The Oresteia, a trilogy of tragedies by Aeschylus – Agamemnon, Choephori (The Libation Bearers), The Eumenides – is first performed in Athens.

460 BC Temple of Zeus, Olympia; Stoa Poikile, Athens.

c.450 BC Discobolus of Myron The original bronze Discobolus (c.430–440 BC) is lost, but the sculpture is known from Roman marble copies such as this one.

447 BC Construction of Parthenon begins.

440 BC Horsemen from the Parthenon Frieze The Parthenon's decorative programme was said to have been designed by Phidias (fl. c.466–400 BC). These blocks come from the frieze that encircled the main rooms.

432 BC Parthenon completed.

c.420–416 BC Warrior Seated at his Tomb Vases decorated in the white-ground style such as this one date almost exclusively from the 5th century BC.

420 BC Temple of Apollo at Bassae.

400 BC Erechtheum Construction of the Heraion, Argolis.

385 BC Plato founds his school at the Academy in Athens.

380 BC Construction of the Temple of Asclepius, Epidauros.

c.400 BC Grave Stele of Hegeso This grave marker from the Dipylon cemetery in Athens is among some of the most beautiful and harmonious funerary reliefs of the Classical period.

148 Timeline

149 Timeline

04

**01.1.11
Timelines:
*Scales of data***

Social Networking Websites is a
double-sided typographic visualization
for an article in *Beef* magazine
in January 2009, which dealt with
networks and communities. It shows
50 major active social networking
websites with their number of users
(font size) and when they were
launched (timeline).

01
Von B und C
Barbara Hahn,
Christine Zimmermann
Social Networking Websites
Beef magazine

253'145'404

M

35'

117'000'000

Habb

90'000'000

Frie

80'000'000

hi5

O

67'000'000

51'000'000

Reunior

50'000'000

Classmates

36'000'

Ne

35'000'000

Linked

27'000'000

Xanga

20'000'000

BlackPlanet

19'000'000

Friends Reunited

22'000'000

Skyrock

21'000'000

Fotolog

24'000'0

ast.fm

ime

17'

LiveJournal

DeviantART

Plaxo

Multiply

13'000'000

Badoo

WAYN

XING

Viadeo

Care2

Trombi

1995 1996 1997 1998 1999 2000 2001 2002 2003 2004

34

ySpac
acebo
indows Liv

ster

ged

ixster

0'000'000
Bebo
0'000'000
29'000'000 Odnoklassniki
V Kontakte

17'000'000 15'000'000
Sonico Geni
Nasza-klasa
diVZ

006   2007   2008   2009

01.1.12
Timelines:
Sense of scale

One Million is a compendium of random statistics, inspired by author Hendrik Hertzberg's impulse to make a newsworthy, large and abstract number more concrete. Think Studio NYC designed the new updated and revised edition. The plan of the book is simple: 200 pages; 5000 dots to a page. The result: one million dots. Notes that correspond to occasional numbers provide unusual and informative historical, political, anatomical and sociological information that helps to reinforce the concept.

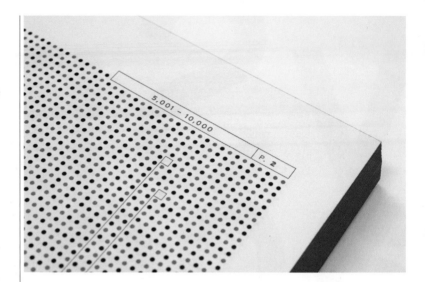

01
Think Studio, NYC
Herb Thornby, John Clifford
One Million
By Hendrik Hertzberg
Abrams Image

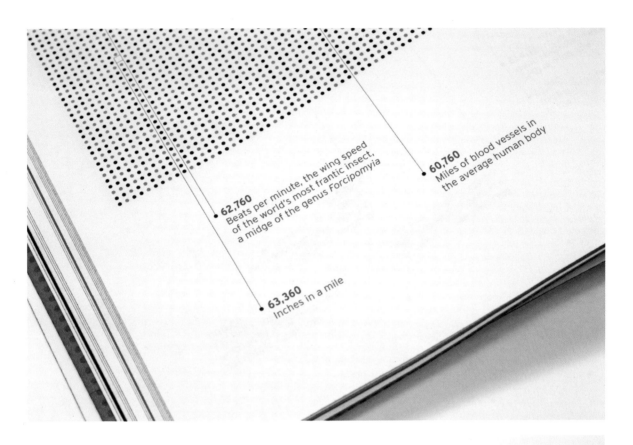

62,760
Beats per minute, the wing speed
of the world's most frantic insect,
a midge of the genus Forcipomyia

60,760
Miles of blood vessels in
the average human body

63,360
Inches in a mile

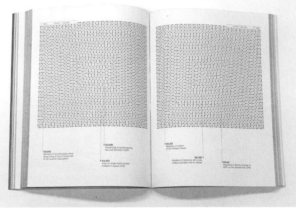

01.1.13
Timelines:
Time sensitive

Self-Confidence Produces Fine Results
is a time-consuming and time-sensitive
installation featuring 10,000 bananas,
which graphically illustrates the
passage of time. Yellow bananas for
the background and unripened green
bananas are used for the lettering.
Over the course of several days the
letters will disapear as the green
bananas ripen and turn yellow. As
time goes by, the yellow background
will turn brown and the lettering will
remain yellow, until some days later
everything will turn to mush.

01
Sagmeister Inc.
Art direction:
Stefan Sagmeister
Design: Richard The,
Joe Shouldice
*Self-Confidence Produces
Fine Results*
A time-based statement at
Deitch Projects, New York

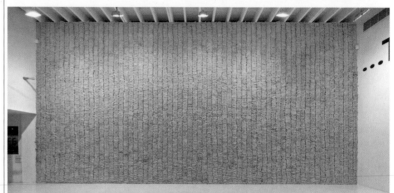

01.2.1
Counting methods:
Timed intervals

Timelines can be graphically illustrated to communicate the passing of time as in this poster by Karin von Ompteda for a one-day seminar, *Visualisation Research*.

A time bar runs down its left side, showing every minute of the talks held during the day. Semicircular arcs are used to illustrate graphically the duration of each talk by increasing in size according to the length of each one, allowing the schedule to be easily read. The times on the left edge are printed larger to represent the beginning of a series of talks, and smaller to represent talks within a session. Small semicircles represent the length of each talk, and larger ones connect related speakers and all talks within a session.

01
Karin von Ompteda
Visualisation Research
Seminar poster

VISU
TION
RESEA
CA&D

10:30

10:40

Karin von Omp
PhD Candidate CA&D
InfoVis: Integrating Scientific and Typographic Knowledge

11:00

Alistair Nash
MPhil Candidate CA&D
Visualisation and Branding

11:20

Matthew Flintham
PhD Candidate CA&D
Geovisualisation and Military Landscapes

11:40

Rachel Pedder-Smith
PhD Candidate CA&D
Natural and Scientific Botanical Illustration

12:00

Manuel Lima
Interaction Designer, Researcher and Founder of VisualComplexity.com
Research Methods Course
Guest Speaker
Lecture Theatre 1

Sara De Bondt
ing Lecturer CA&D / Seminar Respondent

scussion

01.2.2
Counting methods:
Passage of time

Blanka-Helvetica 50 is a poster, graphics and invitation for *Helvetica 50*, an exhibition that celebrated 50 years of the ubiquitous typeface. Fifty designers were invited to take part in the show, each of whom illustrated one of the 50 years from 1957 to 2007. Build's 1969 depicted the historic Neil Armstrong quote 'One small step...'. Their invitation to the exhibition breaks the 50-year period down into seconds, minutes, hours and days.

An editorial feature by Stapelberg & Fritz charts the history of the VW Passat and combines period shots of the car through the years with oversized numeric data.

Design Project's promotional poster for Fedrigoni's new range of Arcoprint papers was produced in two colour ways and makes a feature of the available weights (from 90–350 gsm).

01
Build
Blanka-Helvetica 50
Exhibition invite

02
Build
Blanka-Helvetica 50
Poster

03
Stapelberg & Fritz
The New Passat
Driving Experience
EVW Passat Magazine

04
Design Project
Arcoprint by Fedrigoni
Promotional paper sampler

01

21.07.1969.02:56:15UTC

02

03

Arcoprint—
New limited
edition paper
sampler

Leeds
14 07 2010

90

02.
Data

02.1.1
Quantification:
Proportional divisions

In the Audi *Encounters* magazine, blocks of solid colour represent the various constituent elements used in the construction of the Audi A4 car. The weight of each material is given, and its percentage in the total construction. The limited number of different materials illustrates the recyclability of the car.

The *Audi A8* book features section dividers printed on thick white tracing paper with chapter numbers reversed out of a solid white ink. As in *Encounter*, the book features tonal percentages of the car's material construction.

01
Stapelberg & Fritz
Encounter
The Audi   environmental
magazine

02
Stapelberg & Fritz
Audi A8
Promotional book
for the Audi A8

01

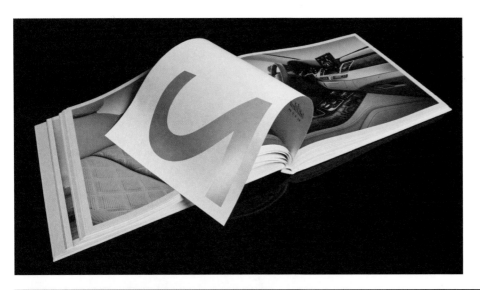

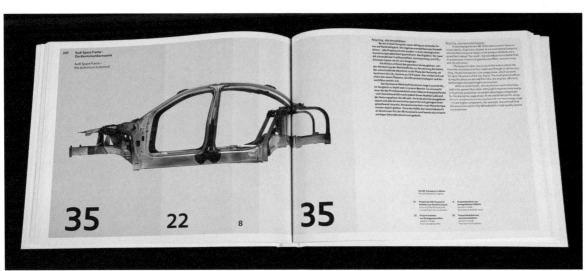

02.1.2
Quantification:
Intersections and networks

Believed to be the most geometrically complex and aesthetically beautiful structure in mathematics, the 4_21 polytope illustrated in *Real Magick in Theory and Practise* is the algebraic form at the centre of a universal theory of everything. It is commonly referred to as E8 since the vectors of its root system lie in eight-dimensional Euclidean space. Its subsumed dimension within dimension structure creates a staggeringly complex 248 symmetrical lattice that predicts all known particles and forces in the universe as it twists and folds in space–time. The limited edition poster is silk-screen-printed in black with 23-carat gold foil and gold powder gilding on a clear polypropylene sheet.

The illustration/infographic for the *New York magazine 00s Issue* is a comment on the development of social networking over the past decade. Each line represents 120,000 registered users on Facebook (black), Myspace (yellow), LinkedIn (purple), Twitter (red), Bebo (green) and Ning (blue).

01
The Luxury of Protest
*Real Magick in Theory
and Practise*
Limited edition poster

02
Studio8
*The 00s Issue
New York magazine*

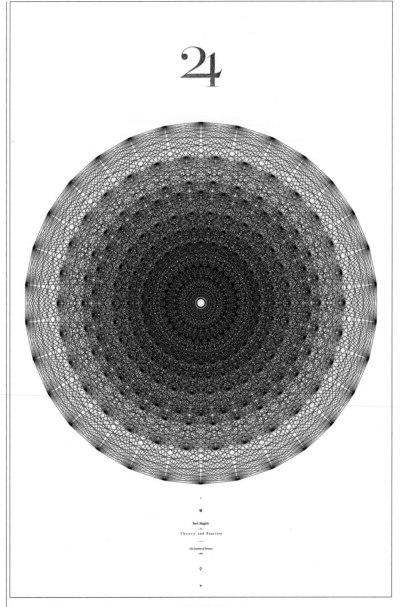

01

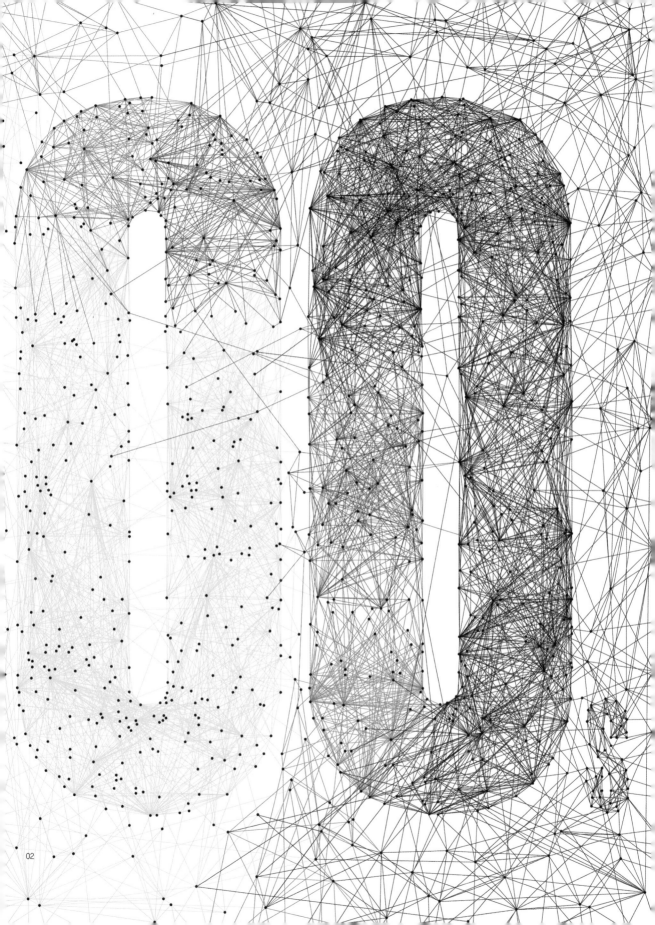

02.1.3
Quantification:
Hard facts

2Dots is a commemorative poster for the 61st anniversary of the nuclear attacks on Hiroshima and Nagasaki. The poster is graphically subdued to represent the sombre nature of the subject matter: single colour, minimal graphics, statistical list of information and spatial arrangement of type elements. The two dots are hand-drawn in matt white paint marker to contrast with the glass-like hyperglossy plastic medium. These dots represent a number of different concepts: the two bombings, us/them, nuclear fission... They symbolize the human tragedy of the bombings and add a notable rough contrast to the clean type treatment.

The *A_B_ Peace & Terror Etc. The Computational Aesthetics of Love & Hate* project is a dual-sided poster that displays a geopolitical survey of the 192 member states of the United Nations. The A_ side displays measures of peace, while the B_ side shows measures of terror. For each of the *A_B_* measures, the graph is divided into three rings (three separate indexes for peace and three separate indexes for terror) which are individual quantitative measures obtained from researchers working in the field of geopolitics. The quantitative variation for the peace and terror measures is represented as variation in line thickness: thin line = low value, thick line = high value.

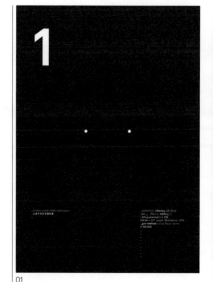

01

02

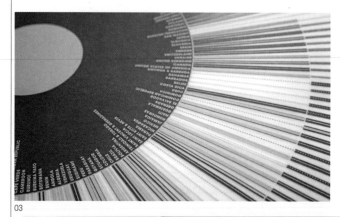

03

04

01, 02
The Luxury of Protest
2Dots
Limited edition poster for the
Hiroshima/Nagasaki War
Museum

03, 04, 05
The Luxury of Protest
A_B_Peace & Terror etc.
*The Computational Aesthetic
of Love & Hate*
Limited edition poster

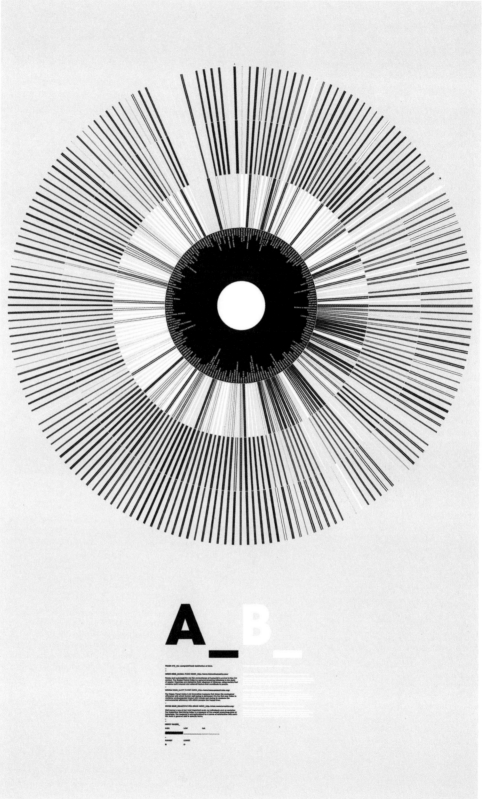

The graph for *Maths Dreamed Universe* was created using generative Python code, and maps numbers 0 to 100,001 arranged in a logarithmic spiral. The form of the spiral is determined by the golden-angle subtension of a circle that distributes numbers from the centre (0) to the outer edge (100,001). The pattern that results is frequently found in nature, as in plants, and has been documented since Archimedes' time. The spiral reveals the visual relationships of elemental numbers and the aesthetic beauty of mathematical equations.

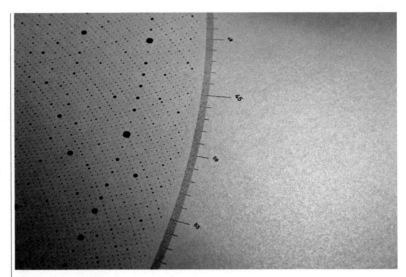

01
The Luxury of Protest
Maths Dreamed Universe
The quantitative visualization
of the manner in which
elemental forms in nature
order themselves

MATHEMATICS IS THE LANGUAGE OF NATURE – THE GRAPH SHOWS THE MAPPING OF NUMBERS 0 TO 100,001 ARRANGED IN A SPIRAL COORDINATE SPACE – THE PATTERN FOLLOWS THE GOLDEN ANGLE SECTIONING OF A CIRCLE WHERE DOTS REPRESENT UNIQUE NUMBER VALUES – VOGEL'S FLORET MODEL ACCURATELY DESCRIBES THE ARRANGEMENT OF ELEMENTAL FORMS IN NATURE SUCH AS PLANT ORGANS ON A FLOWER, THE SPIN OF TROPICAL CYCLONES AND THE FORMATION OF GALAXIES _

MATHS
DREAMED UNI – 0 to 100,001
VERSE.

—

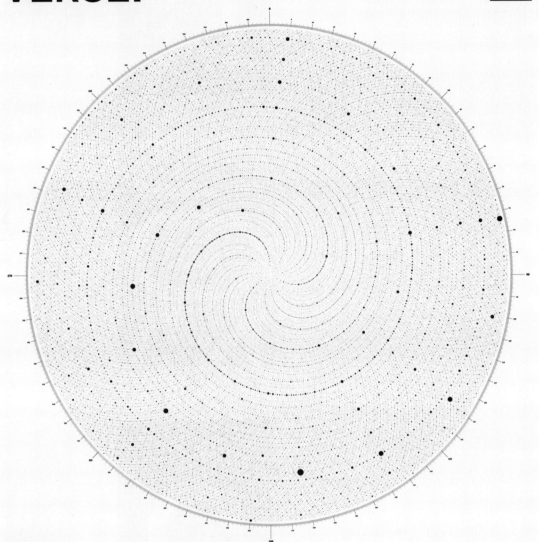

Eq:
r=√n, θ=(2nπ)/φ²

—

02.1.4
Quantification:
Natural forms and order

At This Rate is a booklet produced
for the San Francisco-based charity
Rainforest Action Network (RAN), in
collaboration with photographer Giles
Revell, to raise awareness of the
destruction of the Amazon rainforest.

Each booklet is made from only one
sheet of FSC-certified paper, and folds
out from the cover into a 12-page
concertina, maximizing sheet usage
and minimizing waste.

Each spread includes vital data about
the rainforest, and numbers bleed
off the pages, forming an extreme
contrast with the rest of the text and
the delicacy of the images.

The poster *2060*, again produced in
collaboration with Giles Revell, pairs a
delicate skeletal photographic image
with a bold large-scale numeric title.

02
Studio8
At This Rate
Booklet for the Rainforest
Action Network

03
Studio8
2060
Poster for the Rainforest Action
Network

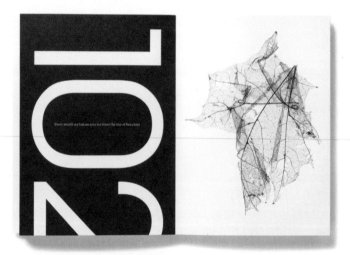

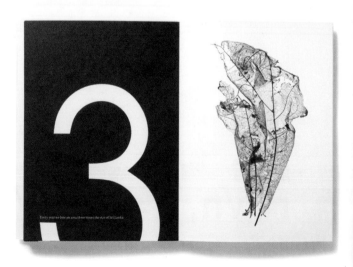

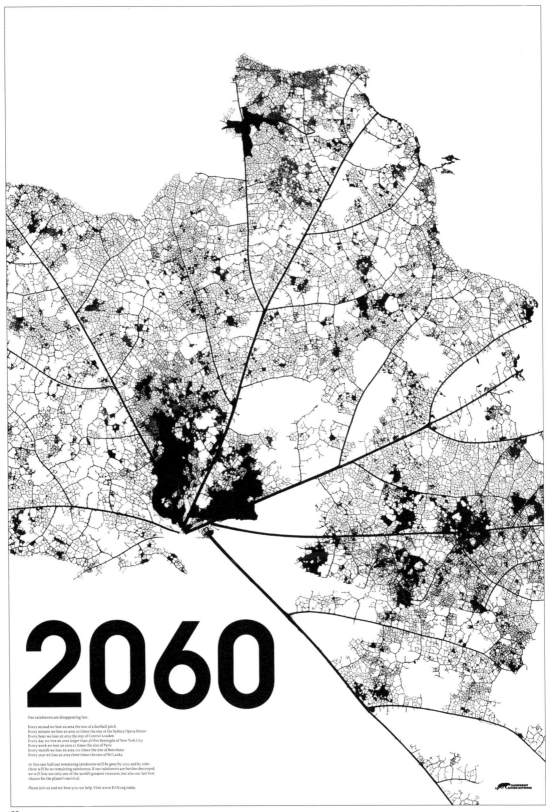

2060

Our rainforests are disappearing fast.

Every second we lose an area the size of a football pitch
Every minute we lose an area 20 times the size of the Sydney Opera House
Every hour we lose an area the size of Central London
Every day we lose an area larger than all five boroughs of New York City
Every week we lose an area 21 times the size of Paris
Every month we lose an area 101 times the size of Barcelona
Every year we lose an area three times the size of Sri Lanka

At this rate half our remaining rainforests will be gone by 2025 and by 2060
there will be no remaining rainforests. If our rainforests are further destroyed,
we will lose not only one of the world's greatest treasures, but also our last best
chance for the planet's survival.

Please join us and see how you can help. Visit www.RAN.org today.

RAINFOREST
ACTION NETWORK

02.1.5
Quantification:
Scale and movement

Visualizing different aspects of the cultural industry and design economy in Berlin, *Business Turnover Berlin 2007* compares the overall economy (G), overall cluster (C), culture economy (K) and design economy (D) in Berlin in 2007.

Design Scene Berlin features 83 located places on the design scene.

Each category – studio, institution, museum, etc. – is indentified by a coloured star. Each venue is represented by a number and its locality in a neighbourhood is marked with a coloured line in such a manner that a representative grid is generated for the relevant area. The more dense the grid, the more venues there are in a district. The locations of the venues form the specific coloured and dense patterns of the diverse districts.

Development of the Berlin Cluster illustrates the growth in creative sectors from 2000 to 2007. The pale grey titles are from 2000 and the black titles from 2007. A vertical scale shows the number of companies and a horizontal scale represents sales. The sector title moves vertically and to the right to represent growth and also increases in size.

01
Von B und C
Barbara Hahn,
Christine Zimmermann
Business turnover Berlin 2007
Form magazine

02
Von B und C
Barbara Hahn,
Christine Zimmermann
Design Scene Berlin
Form magazine

03
Von B und C
Barbara Hahn,
Christine Zimmermann
Development of the Berlin cluster communication, media, creative industries from 2000–07
Form magazine

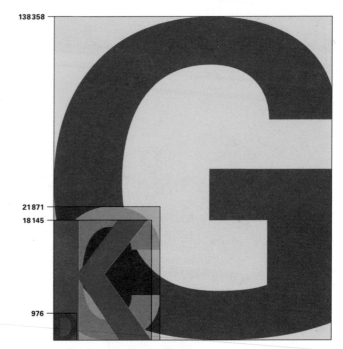

Wirtschaftsumsätze Berlin 2007
Business turnover Berlin 2007

138358

21871
18145

976

G = Gesamtwirtschaft / *Overall economy*
C = Gesamtcluster / *Overall cluster*
K = Kulturwirtschaft / *Culture economy*
D = Designwirtschaft / *Design economy*

in Mio. Euro, gerundet / *to the nearest million euros*

01

02

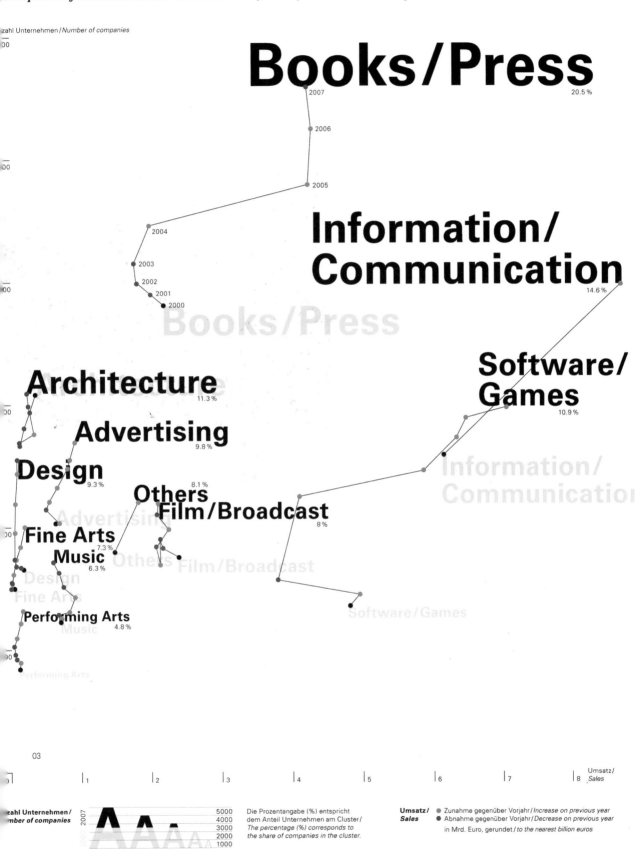

zahl Unternehmen / *Number of companies*

Books/Press
20.5 %

2007
2006
2005
2004
2003
2002
2001
2000

**Information/
Communication**
14.6 %

Books/Press

**Software/
Games**
10.9 %

Architecture
11.3 %

Advertising
9.8 %

Design
9.3 %

Others
8.1 %

Film/Broadcast
8 %

Information/
Communication

Fine Arts
7.3 %

Music
6.3 %

Others Film/Broadcast

Advertising

Design
Fine Arts

Music

Performing Arts
4.8 %

Software/Games

Performing Arts

03

| 0 | | 1 | | 2 | | 3 | | 4 | | 5 | | 6 | | 7 | | 8 | Umsatz/ *Sales* |

zahl Unternehmen /
mber of companies

2007

5000
4000
3000
2000
1000

Die Prozentangabe (%) entspricht
dem Anteil Unternehmen am Cluster/
*The percentage (%) corresponds to
the share of companies in the cluster.*

Umsatz/
Sales

● Zunahme gegenüber Vorjahr/*Increase on previous year*
● Abnahme gegenüber Vorjahr/*Decrease on previous year*
in Mrd. Euro, gerundet/*to the nearest billion euros*

02.1.6
Quantification:
Visual analysis

For the research project *Visual Atlas of Everyday Life at the Hospital* four independent and innovative visualizations were developed to help represent selected organizational and communicative subprocesses within the patient process at Berne University Hospital. As a result, working processes and structures can be more clearly represented within the hospital, and can be analyzed and hence managed more efficiently.

The data for the four visualized subprocesses had already been collected for process analysis projects at the hospital's department for quality management. About 90 patients leaving hospital responded to a questionnaire in order to certify the level of information in the visualizations and answer important questions concerning their recovery.

01
Von B und C
Barbara Hahn,
Christine Zimmermann
Visual Atlas of Everyday Life at the Hospital
Berne University of the Arts/
Berne University Hospital

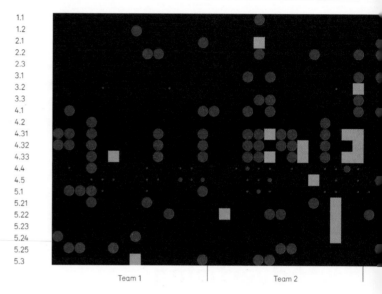

Gesamtansicht

B5 Patientenaustritt

■ sehr gut
informiert

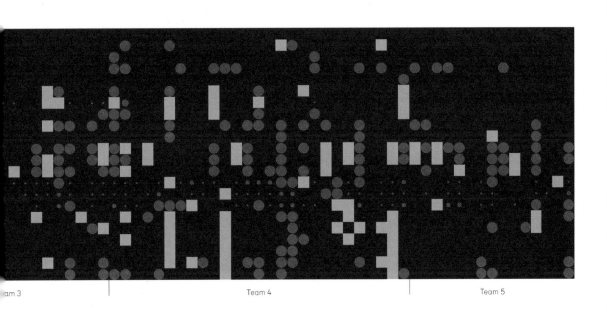

am 3 Team 4 Team 5

miert mittelmässig
informiert

schlecht
informiert

sehr schlecht
informiert

Daten nicht
erhoben

Social Maps shows the social network and communication behaviour (face-to-face, telephone, Skype, e-mail, mail) of seven women (A to G) in the context of the scientific study *Women's Phone.* All communication partners of each of the seven women are placed radially around them. On the five outer circles (one circle for each form of communication) all communication forms that are used with a particular person are highlighted by coloured strokes. The colour indicates the relationship between two people in five steps from warm to cold colours: partner (orange), family (red), friends (violet), acquaintances (purple), colleagues (blue). The thickness of a stroke correlates with the geographical closeness/distance of the people concerned: within a city (thick stroke), a country (medium stroke), the world (thin stroke).

Adjectival Scales shows an analysis of 66 objects that were collected by five individuals in the *Women's Phone* study. The objects were analyzed with regard to 49 characteristics (organic, decorative, small, soft, fleecy, smooth, shiny, eye-catching, aromatic, discreet, harsh, etc.). A matrix (adjectives on X-axis, objects on Y-axis) illustrates through colour coding with three steps of colour intensity whether a characteristic applies to an object highly, partially or not at all. The five people are subtly differentiated through different shades of red from violet to orange.

Women's Phone: **Social Maps**

02

02
Von B und C
Barbara Hahn,
Christine Zimmermann
Women's Phone:
Social Maps
Deutsche Telekom Laboratories

03
Von B und C
Barbara Hahn,
Christine Zimmermann
Women's Phone:
Adjectival Scales
Deutsche Telekom Laboratories

04
Von B und C
Barbara Hahn,
Christine Zimmermann
Women's Phone:
Adjectival Scales
Deutsche Telekom Laboratories

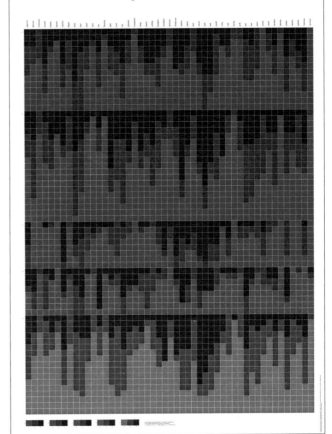

Women's Phone: **Adjektivische Skalen II**

04

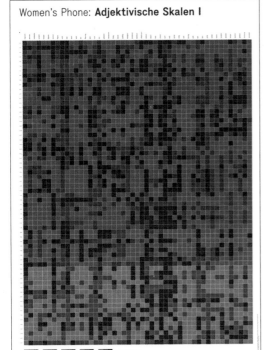

Women's Phone: **Adjektivische Skalen I**

03

02.1.6
Quantification:
Visual analysis

Designers, statisticians, geographers, architects and communications experts all work with data. *Data Visualization Beyond Pie Charts and Bar Graphs* demonstrates how depictive knowledge can be won from data records by means of innovative visualizations beyond conventional graphical representations. In addition to nine developed visualizations, the book contains all the data that was collected during the work process. Using a Japanese bookbinding method, the exterior pages contain the primary material (the data) while the inner pages show the visuals. The latter are perforated so that they can be removed from the body of the book and then unfolded to reveal large-scale posters.

Women's Phone: Formal Aesthetic Analysis illustrates the reference objects found by five individuals as a colour spectrum. The objective of the visual conversion was to condense characteristic features of the three formal aesthetic criteria (form, colour and surface structure).

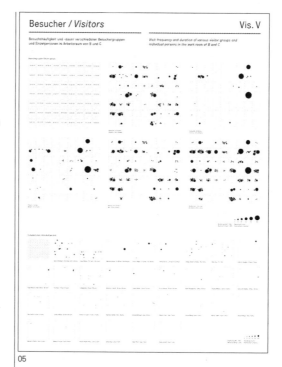

05

06

05
Von B und C
Barbara Hahn,
Christine Zimmermann
Data Visualization Beyond Pie Charts and Bar Graphs
Christoph Merian Verlag

06
Von B und C
Barbara Hahn,
Christine Zimmermann
*Women's Phone:
Formal Aesthetic Analysis*
Deutsche Telekom
Laboratories

07
Von B und C
Barbara Hahn,
Christine Zimmermann
Data Visualization Beyond Pie Charts and Bar Graphs
Christoph Merian Verlag

Zusammenarbeit / *Collaboration*

Vis. IX

Gemeinsame und getrennte Arbeitsphasen von B und C,
nach vier Arbeitsweisen unterschieden

*Mutual and separate work phases of B and C, differentiated
according to four work modes*

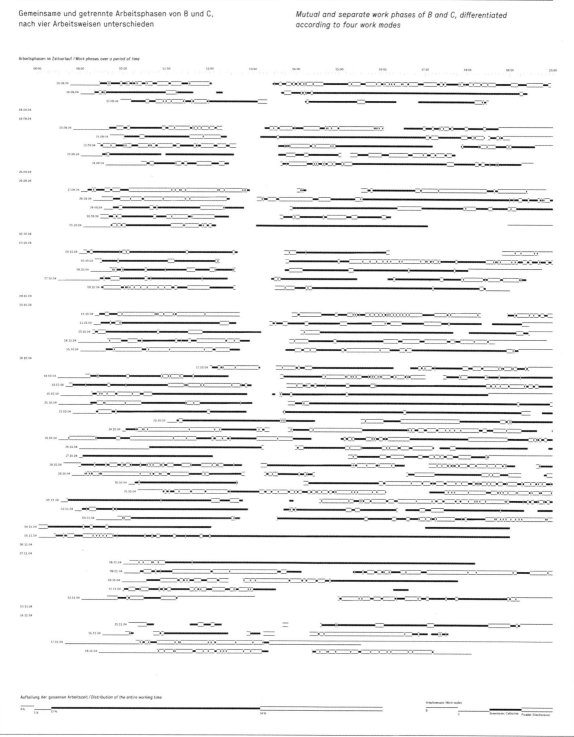

Arbeitsphasen im Zeitverlauf / *Work phases over a period of time*

Aufteilung der gesamten Arbeitszeit / *Distribution of the entire working time*

02.1.7
Quantification:
Time based

Unix time is a system for describing
points in time, defined as the number
of seconds that have elapsed since
the Unix epoch – midnight Universal
Time Coordinated (UTC) 1 January
1970. Any point in time can be
converted into its running second total.
On Friday 13 February 2009 at 23:31:30
Unix time reached 1 234 567 890.
The Unix Time Stamp series of prints
was created to mark this event and a
selection of other key calendar dates
in 2009, such as the inauguration
of President Barack Obama on 20
January, 2009.

01

01
Jason Delahunty
CodyDelahunty
*The Inauguration of
President Barack Obama*
Poster

02
Jason Delahunty
CodyDelahunty
*Unix Time Stamp
Solstice*
Poster

03
Jason Delahunty
CodyDelahunty
*Unix Time Stamp
1 234 567 890*
Poster

02

1 234 567 890
23:31:30
13-02-2009

Edition
1 of 25

Unix Time Stamp
Progression

Arrival
Graphic Design

03

A report for the London Mayor's Fund highlights statistics for the borough of Shoreditch. This spread focuses on the communities in the area, using simple iconic human forms and a vibrant palette of colours to illustrate the ethic mix in the different sectors.

01
April
London Mayor's Fund
Report

THE LOCAL COMMUNITIES

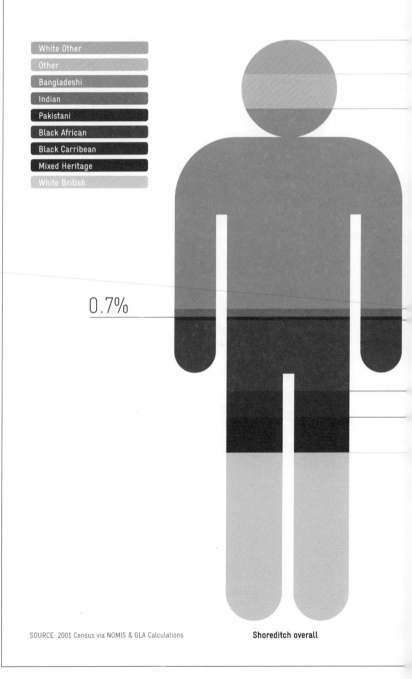

White Other
Other
Bangladeshi
Indian
Pakistani
Black African
Black Carribean
Mixed Heritage
White British

0.7%

SOURCE: 2001 Census via NOMIS & GLA Calculations

Shoreditch overall

Shoreditch has a wide range of communities from the Bangladeshi community of Bethnal Green, to the Turkish community of Hackney and the traditional white working class estates of Central Street and Finsbury. Other communities include the Afro-Caribbean, Kurdish and Somalian communities.

Of all children living in the area:
- 34% are from the Bangladeshi community, with a strong representation (up to 70%) in the eastern wards of Tower Hamlets
- 29% are white British, with a higher concentration in the Islington wards (55%)

- 17% are from the African-Caribbean community, with up to 35% in the Hackney wards
- 42% of children are Muslim, 35% Christian
- 14% of children are born outside the UK

Shoreditch is therefore a 'Community of Communities', and a one-size-fits-all approach to problem solving is not feasible. To deliver on our mission, we have resolved to work in partnership with the local Shoreditch communities. These comprise faith groups, residents associations, traders associations, schools, etc. This means that the local priorities and needs of the community are reflected in the programmes that we develop.

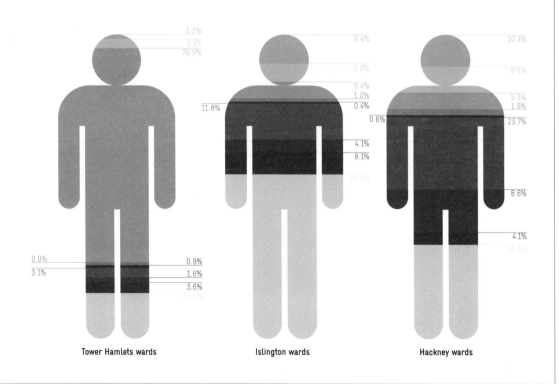

Tower Hamlets wards   Islington wards   Hackney wards

02.2.1
Statistics:
Touch screen

The Times' iPad edition is supported by an ongoing series of interactive graphics. Shown here are a series of infographics depicting the North/South health divide in England, an infographic illustrating the huge growth of the United Kingdom's national debt since 2000 and a timeline for the 70th anniversary of the Battle of Britain.

01

01
Applied Works
The Times iPad edition
Battle of Britain timeline

02
Applied Works
The Times iPad edition
Pillars of Spending

03
Applied Works
The Times iPad edition
North/South health divide

04, 05
Applied Works
The Times iPad edition
The Wall of Debt

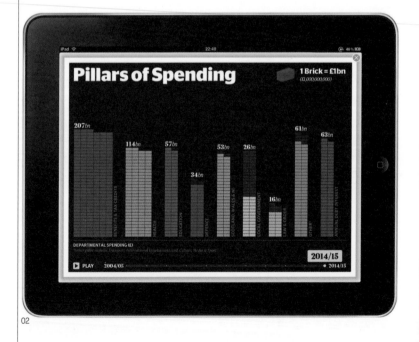

02

03

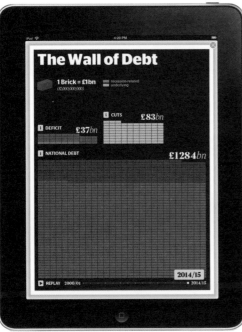

04

The Wall of Debt

1 Brick = £1bn
(£1,000,000,000)
■ recession-related
■ underlying

i NATIONAL DEBT   £311bn

2000/01

▶ PLAY   2000/01 •   2014/15

05

02.2.2
Statistics:
Data explosions

Financial data from Slovakia's Department of Culture and Serbia's Ministry of Culture is visualized for the visibledata.info project.

Amoeba is a classic column chart, but instead of displaying values on a straight axis the columns are convoluted to form a circle with the spikes representing values.

Big Bang is more of a visual than a functional approach to visualizing data. Each of the randomly positioned circles represents an actual value and the central circle, or the source of the explosion, has an area equal to the areas of all the white circles combined.

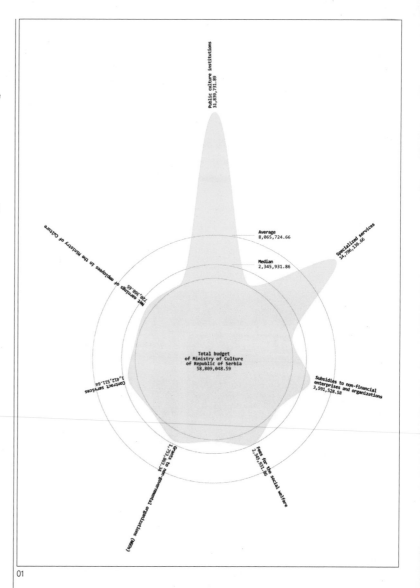

Public culture institutions
31,839,731.89

Average
8,065,724.66

Median
2,345,931.86

Specialized services
14,796,136.66

Total budget
of Ministry of Culture
of Republic of Serbia
58,809,048.59

Subsidies to non-financial
enterprises and organizations
3,591,528.58

Net earnings of employees in the Ministry of Culture
790,388.65

Contract services
1,413,511.64

Fees for the social welfare
2,363,921.86

Grants to non-government organizations (NGO)
1,751,639.34

01

01
Ondrej Jób
Amoeba
visibledata.info

02
Ondrej Jób
Big Bang
visibledata.info

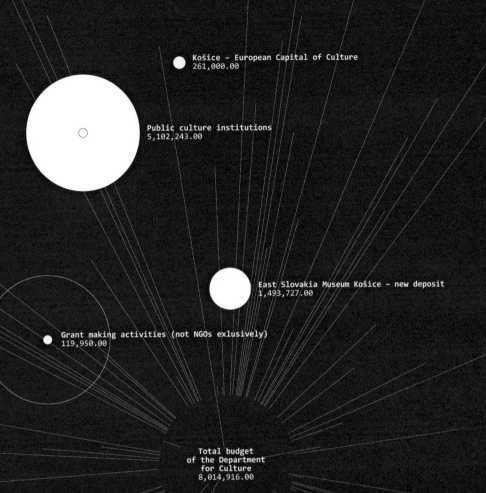

Košice – European Capital of Culture
261,000.00

Public culture institutions
5,102,243.00

East Slovakia Museum Košice – new deposit
1,493,727.00

Grant making activities (not NGOs exlusively)
119,950.00

Total budget
of the Department
for Culture
8,014,916.00

Cultural activities and cultural heritage
293,953.00

East Slovakia Museum Košice –
reconstruction of the historical building
744,043.00

02.2.3
Statistics:
Concept of scale

Everyone Ever in the World is a
visual representation of the number
of people who have lived versus
the number who have been killed
as a result of wars, massacres and
genocide during the recorded history
of humankind. The visualization uses
the existing paper area and paper
loss (a die-cut circle) to represent the
concepts of life and death respectively.
The total number of people who have
lived during the recorded history
of humankind was estimated to be
approximately 77.6 billion, represented
in the poster as the total paper area
(650mm x 920mm). The number of
people killed in conflicts was collated
from historical source books and
totalled approximately 969 million. The
timescale encompasses 3200 BC to AD
2009 – a period of over five millennia
that saw 1100-plus conflicts.

The sequence of dots to the top left
of the graph shows the dramatic
increase in the number of conflicts
over the past five millennia (left to
right: 3000 BC to AD 2000); the most
recent 1000 years are the most
violent. The large dot below the graph
represents the next 1000 years and
a predicted startling increase in the
frequency of human conflict.

01

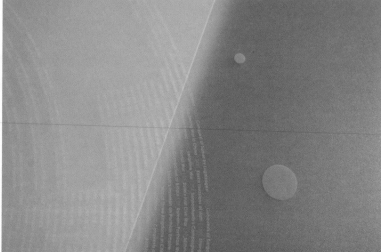

02

01, 04
The Luxury of Protest
Everyone Ever in the World
(First Edition)
Large-format poster with
die cuts screen printed in gloss
transparent ink on black plastic

02
The Luxury of Protest
Everyone Ever in the World
(Second Edition)
Large-format poster with
die cuts screen printed gloss
milk-white ink on clear plastic

03
The Luxury of Protest
Everyone Ever in the World
(Third Edition)
Large-format poster with
laser engraved and laser cut
on cotton paper

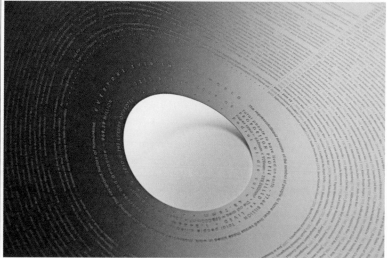

03

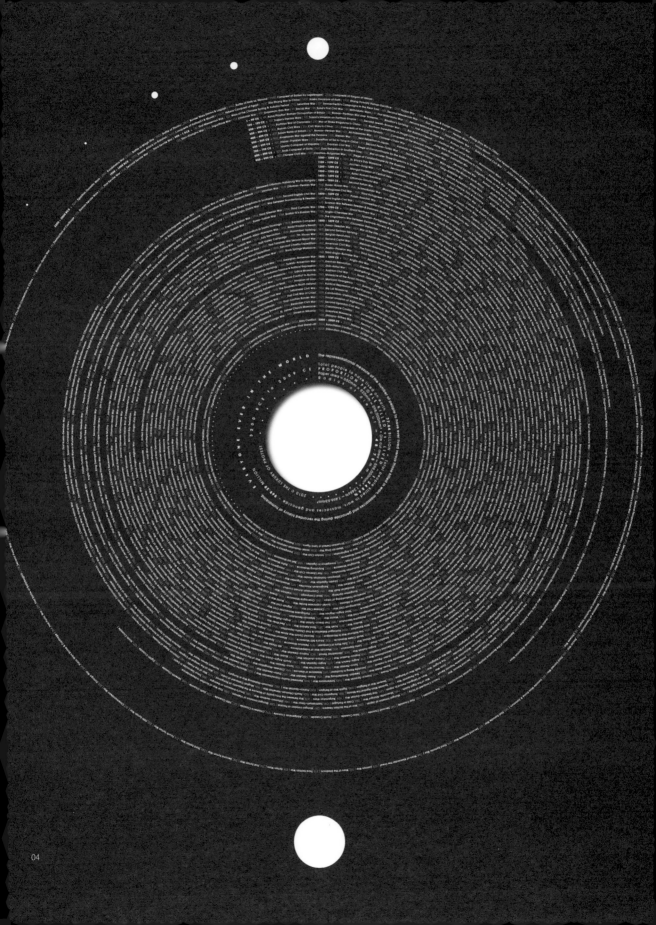

02.2.4
Statistics:
Revolution

The Universal Declaration is a graphic
call to arms. The project is a series
of five designer-initiated posters that
address articles from the Universal
Declaration of Human Rights and
deals directly with rights of protest
and free speech. Elemental circles are
used to express the essence of each
article through the contrast of a single
graphite-pencil dot and standard black
dots. The graphite dot represents
different ideas on each poster, such
as freedom of personal expression for
'the right to free thought...' article.

01
The Luxury of Protest
The Universal Declaration
Poster series

THE RIGHT TO FREEDOM FROM PERSE-CUTION

THE LUXURY OF PROTEST .COM

02.2.5
Statistics:
Visual analysis

Concept and design of the visualizations for *Questions*, the magazine published by the Julius Baer bank on the occasion of its second investment conference, 'Change for a better world – are green investments sustainable?'. The illustrative data visualizations depict facts concerning energy consumption, water shortage, quality or demand and thus visually complete the editorial section.

01
Von B und C
Barbara Hahn,
Christine Zimmermann
Questions
Julius Baer bank

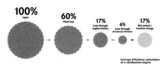

Annual consumption, annual renewable resources and fossil energy resources
World Energy Council, BP Statistical Energy Review, 2009

The solar revolution

The energy efficiency solution

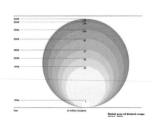

Average efficiency calculation of a combustion engine
Julius Baer, 2011

> "Two-thirds of primary energy input is lost."

Agriculture – how to meet tomorrow's demand

by Moritz Baumann
Julius Baer

Apart from cyclical swings and regional shortages, food prices, when adjusted for deflation, have declined over the past decades.

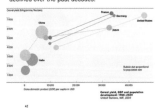

Cereal yield, GDP and population development 1960–2009
United Nations, IMF, 2009

Biotech

Global area of biotech crops
ISAAA, 2009

What about the clean energy milieu in Switzerland?

by Thomas P. Schmid
Capital Dynamics

The need for, and importance of, clean energy infrastructure is increasing in Switzerland.

Drivers for the shift from fossil to renewable energy and the increasing significance of energy efficiency are comparable to those within the European Union and around the globe. Lacking access to the sea, Switzerland is dependent upon imports of non-renewable energy for 81% of its total energy consumption. Thus, a secure and broadly diversified energy supply is crucial for the country.

The Swiss government established national CO_2 legislation in 1999 and signed the Kyoto Protocol, an international agreement linked to the United Nations Framework Convention on Climate Change in 2003. Switzerland made a commitment to reduce its greenhouse gas emissions during the 2008 to 2012 period by 8%, as compared to 1990 levels. The implementation of the reduction targets is based on the 1999 CO_2 legislation, energy legislation and a programme called 'EnergieSchweiz' that is related to the energy legislation. The Climate Cent Foundation is a voluntary programme by Swiss industry aimed at efficient climate protection under the CO_2 law.

The Climate Cent Foundation committed to the demonstrable reduction of 12 million tonnes of CO_2 over the 2008 to 2012 period, of which at least

two million tonnes of CO_2 must be reduced within Switzerland. Under the terms of the Kyoto Protocol, over this period, Switzerland must reduce its emissions by 21 million tonnes of CO_2 compared to what is now five times its 1990 level. The Climate Cent Foundation fulfilled 60% of the Swiss targets by buying emission reduction allowances. By 31 December 2009, the Climate Cent Foundation had received contracts for the reduction of 2.83 million tonnes of CO_2 within Switzerland over the 2008 to 2012 period, and dedicated CHF 485 million to their purchase. By the same date, contracts had been signed for the purchase of 11.9 million Kyoto certificates (each certificate being equivalent to one reduced tonne of CO_2) at a total cost of CHF 253 million.

In Switzerland, the CO_2 Act forms the basis for climate policy and regulates reduction measures until the end of 2012. It must therefore be revised to cover 2013 and beyond. The Federal Council is now in the process of submitting a dispatch on the revision to Parliament. This draft on the revision of the CO_2 Act is planned as an indirect counter-proposal to the popular federal initiative 'For a healthy climate'. By 2020, Switzerland plans to reduce its greenhouse gas emissions by at least 20%, compared to 1990 emission levels.

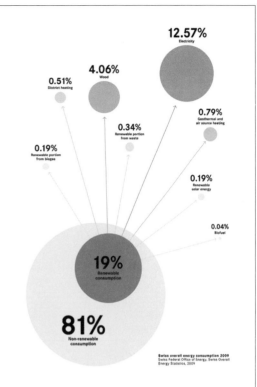

12.57%
Electricity

4.06%
Wood

0.51%
District heating

0.79%
Geothermal and air source heating

0.34%
Renewable portion from waste

0.19%
Renewable portion from biogas

0.19%
Renewable solar energy

0.04%
Biofuel

19%
Renewable consumption

81%
Non-renewable consumption

Swiss overall energy consumption 2009
Swiss Federal Office of Energy, Swiss Overall Energy Statistics, 2009

16

---

they prove to markedly reduce the need for chemical fertilisers or pesticides, and allow less use of machinery and equipment, or perhaps require not as much irrigation? Given the challenges global agriculture faces to boost output in the decades ahead, and the fact that a few important food-producing countries, such as the United States, Brazil, India and China, already are increasingly using these new, modified crops, it appears likely that biotechnology will play a central role in the agricultural production of the 21st century.

Fertilisers

The hunt for higher yields requires soils with the necessary nutrients for plant growth. To maintain productivity, nutrients taken out of the soil at harvest must be replenished. Fertilisers containing nitrogen, phosphorus and potash, as well as other minerals providing nutrients, are a key part of today's agricultural production. While in the developed world fertiliser use has remained fairly stable, such is clearly not the case in major developing producers like India

and China where application of fertilisers still is below potential and not well balanced in terms of how the various ingredients are mixed. This makes it harder for farmers to achieve higher yields. Over the past years, we have seen strong growth in fertiliser demand in developing regions, which is set to continue. Fertilisers wrongly applied, however, pose significant hazards to the environment and to soil quality, and can also affect water resources, damage that might be irreversible. Such adverse outcomes have put severe

> "Over the past years, we have seen strong growth in fertiliser demand in developing regions, which is set to continue."

strain on the ecosystems in the past. Yet environmental damage associated with fertilisers can be substantially reduced if these are applied correctly based on plant needs, while the benefits can be fully exploited. The challenge in the future will be to mitigate the potential damage to the environment that may result from fertilisers, even as the volumes in use are set to grow. Comprehensive solutions to manage nutrients include speciality fertilisers targeted to specific needs of plants and soil. Making professional advice available to farmers is also key. These aspects will play a major part in sustainable use of fertilisers in the future.

Agricultural equipment

In developed countries, mechanised production has largely replaced human labour in agriculture. This has facilitated large-scale farming and has allowed for enormous gains in productivity. While countries in the developing world are still in the process

of introducing more machinery as they increasingly industrialise, a large share of the work in many of these places is still done by hand labour and animal strength. More widespread use of machinery to produce food crops in these countries is needed as urbanisation and jobs in other sectors attract rural dwellers away from the land. The trend towards substituting mechanisation for backbreaking human labour is driving demand for basic, small-scale equipment. This is true especially in parts of the developing world where farms are still relatively small, and thus unsuited for heavy machinery. Meanwhile in the developed world, changes underway include 'precision farming practices'. GPS-navigated machinery and measuring soil quality via satellite are some of the ways farming and IT are being combined to allow for more precise applications of pesticides, water and fertilisers. Besides potential to increase profitability of production and reduce volatility of crop yields, such techniques can reduce the adverse effects on the environment caused by agriculture.

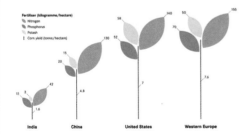

Animal 30%

Hand 35%

Animal 20%

Hand 25%

Tractor 35%

Tractor 55%

2000
2030
Year

Developing world – expected change in agricultural power mix
United Nations, 2003

Fertiliser (kilogramme/hectare)
Nitrogen
Phosphorus
Potash
Corn yield (tonne/hectare)

India 15 3 1.6

China 20 43 4.9 92 130

United States 58 70 140 7

Western Europe 50 155 7.6

Fertiliser usage and corn yield
International Fertilizer Industry Association, 2009

44

45

02.2.6
Statistics:
Data rich

In the early 1990s the Dutch Ministry of Housing, Spatial Planning and the Environment published a supplement to the fourth report on spatial planning. This policy document achieved fame and notoriety under its Dutch acronym, Vinex. In its wake, hundreds of thousands of dwellings were erected throughout the Netherlands in what became known as Vinex districts. Sometimes eulogized, often vilified, they have always been a source of debate. The *Vinex Atlas* gives the first in-depth account of the entire Vinex stock, describing 52 districts with the aid of aerial views taken in the mid-1990s, plans, site data and recent on-site photographs.

01
Joost Grootens
Vinex Atlas
010 Publishers

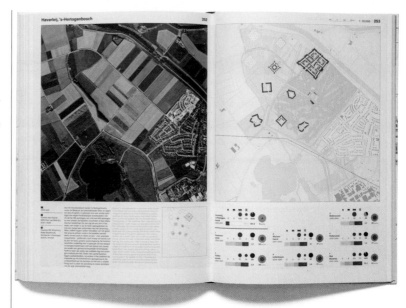

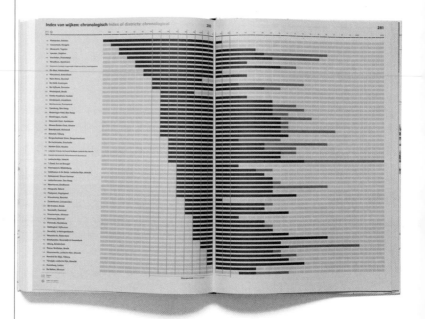

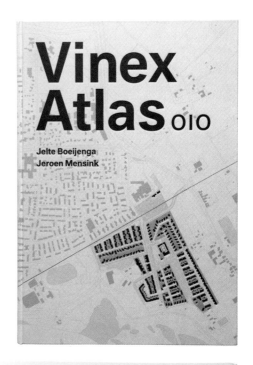

Vinex Atlas 010

Jelte Boeijenga
Jeroen Mensink

STADSGEWEST HILVERSUM
Blaricum, Bussum, Hilversum, Huizen, Laren, Muiden, Naarden, Weesp, Wijdemeren

STADSGEWEST ALKMAAR
Alkmaar, Bergen, Graft-De Rijp, Heerhugowaard, Heiloo, Langedijk, Schermer

STADSGEWEST HAARLEM-IJMOND
Bennebroek, Beverwijk, Bloemendaal, Castricum, Haarlem, Haarlemmerliede c.a., Heemskerk, Heemstede, Uitgeest, Velsen, Zandvoort

REGIONAAL ORGAAN AMSTERDAM (ROA)
Aalsmeer, Almere, Amstelveen, Amsterdam, Beemster, Diemen, Edam-Volendam, Haarlemmermeer, Landsmeer, Oostzaan, Ouder-Amstel, Purmerend, Uithoorn, Waterland, Wormerland, Zaanstad, Zeevang

STADSGEWEST LEIDEN-BOLLENSTREEK
Alkemade, Hillegom, Katwijk, Leiden, Leiderdorp, Lisse, Noordwijk, Noordwijkerhout, Oegstgeest, Teylingen, Voorschoten, Zoeterwoude

STADSGEWEST HAAGLANDEN
Delft, Den Haag, Leidschendam-Voorburg, Pijnacker-Nootdorp, Rijswijk, Wassenaar, Zoetermeer

STADSREGIO ROTTERDAM (SRR)
Albrandswaard, Barendrecht, Bernisse, Brielle, Capelle aan den IJssel, Hellevoetsluis, Krimpen aan den IJssel, Lansingerland, Maassluis, Ridderkerk, Rotterdam, Rozenburg, Schiedam, Spijkenisse, Vlaardingen, Westvoorne

02.2.7
Statistics:
Directional

The wayfinding signage system for the Tübingen District Council building utilizes the ceiling space for both directional signage information and statistical data such as distances to other locations.

Average UK Rainfall follows on from the *Hours of Dark* and *Hours of Light* posters (see pages 24–27). The poster features a graph that charts average rainfall in the United Kingdom between 1971 and 2000. The graph itself is styled to resemble a downpour of rain. The bars are plotted directly over the weather stations they relate to, which gives an abstracted map of the UK. Printed black and UV varnish on white stock.

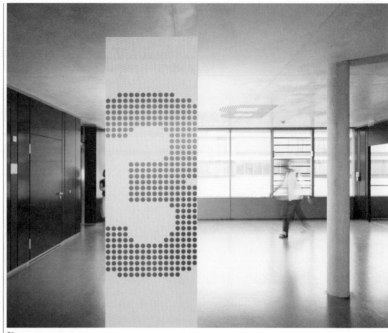

01

01, 02, 03, 04
L2M3 Kommunikationsdesign
*Tübingen District Council
signage system*
Wayfinding system

05
Accept and Proceed
Average UK Rainfall
Limited edition poster

05

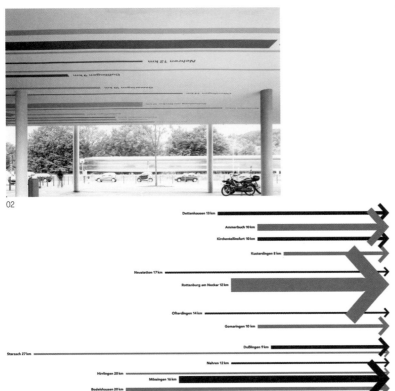

02

03

04

02.2.8
Statistics:
Work flow

Ben Saunders Polar Explorer is a stat-rich website that in 2011 tracked the live progress of North 3, a solo and unsupported North Pole speed record attempt by the explorer and record-breaking long-distance skier. Hourly positional data, a daily updated infographic (displaying latitude, distance per day, sled weight and temperature) and daily blog posts allowed people to follow Saunders' progress over the 36-day expedition.

Work Calendar illustrates the designer's workload over a period of five years. The volume of work is based on the number of e-mails received during the relevant year.

Work Year 2007 is a calendar that shows the designer's volume of work during the course of 2007. Each dot represents one day – the bigger the dot, the greater the workload. Each month of the year has its own colour. All the data used is based on the number of e-mails received each day.

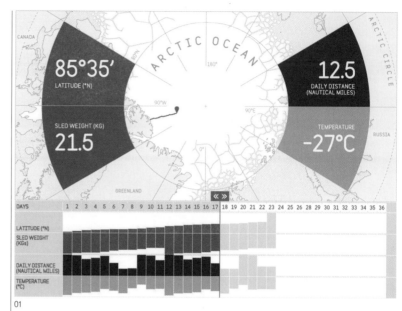

01

01
Applied Works /
Studio8 Design
Ben Saunders Polar Explorer
Information graphics

02
Hörður Lárusson
Work Calendar 04–09
Charts the number of e-mails
received each year

03, 04
Hörður Lárusson
Work Year 2007
Charts the number of e-mails
received each day of the year

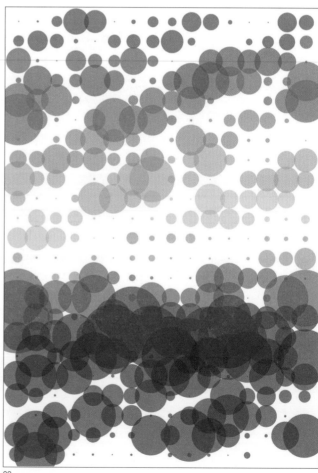

02

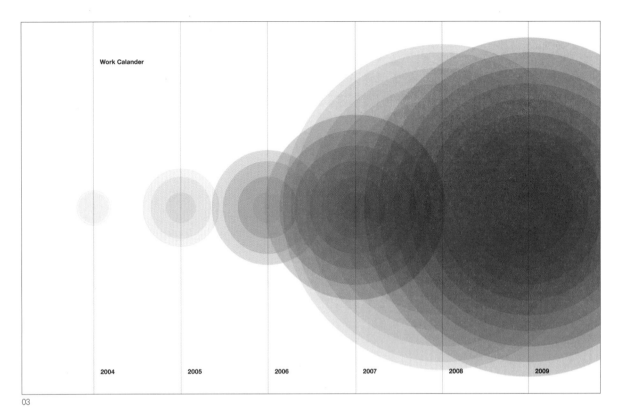

Work Calander

2004   2005   2006   2007   2008   2009

03

2006

2005

04

02.3.1
Report and accounts:
Pie charts

The Media Trust report and accounts designed by Form create an elegant solution to dry accounts information. The pie charts, printed in tints of a single blue, appear large and uncluttered, with discreet annotation printed clear of the roundels. Large-scale numeric data is pulled out into the margins and highlighted to add colour to the report.

The annual report for international specialist insurer Hiscox keeps the colour palette to a minimum, relying on red, grey and black. Likewise, the charts are restrained and minimal.

01
Form
Media Trust
Report and accounts

02
Browns
Hiscox 2010
Annual report and accounts

01

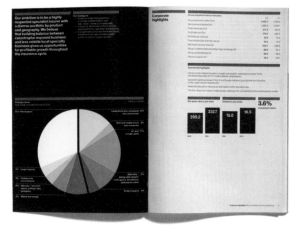
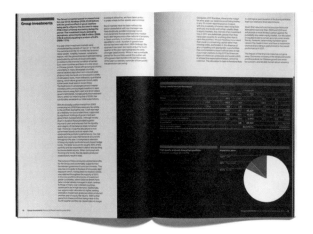
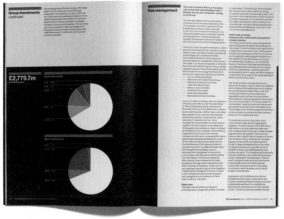

02

Report and accounts:
Bar charts

The Design Council is the United Kingdom's national strategic body for design. The *07/08 Annual Review* designed by Bibliothèque presents three key areas of their policy: competitiveness, sustainability and innovation. Growth across these areas is expressed photographically as opposed to the more conventional diagrammatic approach. The graphs and charts float in a red environment (the Design Council corporate colour) creating an emotive and pictorial element that is usually missing in statistical information.

Stapelberg & Fritz's infographics design for *E&A Magazine* is printed white out of black on cheap newsprint. The raw data is kept simple and the statistical information stripped of all decorative elements, with large pie charts and bold large numbers taking centre stage in the design.

01
Bibliothèque
07/08 Annual Review
The Design Council

02
Stapelberg & Fritz
E&A Magazine
Infographics design

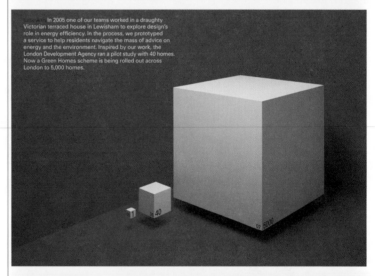

From a standing start in 2004, Designing Demand enabled 124 companies to use design more strategically and effectively. By the end of 2007, 1,556 firms had benefited. On average, for every £1 spent on design, companies who received our intensive mentoring returned a £50 increase in turnover above expected levels.

124   179   489   764

In 2005 one of our teams worked in a draughty Victorian terraced house in Lewisham to explore design's role in energy efficiency. In the process, we prototyped a service to help residents navigate the mass of advice on energy and the environment. Inspired by our work, the London Development Agency ran a pilot study with 40 homes. Now a Green Homes scheme is being rolled out across London to 5,000 homes.

1   40   5000

Hi-tech firms are using design to transform their business. UK companies using the Designing Demand Innovate service found the programme greatly improved their ability to raise money, develop new products and strategies and sharpen their branding.

80% Changed strategic direction
50% Changed skills
65% Changed branding
35% Changed product

Table 1

Household Consumption
Selected Countries

Circa 2000

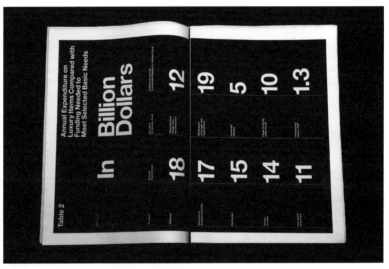

Table 2

Annual Expenditure on
Luxury Items Compared with
Funding Needed to
Meet Selected Basic Needs

In
Billion
Dollars

18	12
17	19
15	5
14	10
11	1.3

Table 3

Consumer Spending
and Population

By
Region

Fig. b

Share of World
Population

in percent

Fig. a

Share of World
Private Consumption
Expenditures

in percent

02.3.3
Report and accounts:
No charts

All pie charts, graphs and other diagrammatic devices were stripped away for the 1979 annual report for the Japanese pharmaceutical company Otsuka. However, the data is far from dull. The sales data is illustrated with the percentages reproduced in comparative scale to each other, with a different colour used for each sector. The cover of a later report for the same company plays with the two zeros taken from the year 2003 as a graphic device to reveal details from the company's operation.

The *Breaking Barriers Report and Summary* for the Active Communities Network by Commercial Art comprises a 72-page academic report that includes a large proportion of tabular information and numbered sections. This numbering system forms the backbone of the report as other visual material is limited.

01
Helmut Schmid
Otsuka Pharmaceutical 1979
Spreads from the annual report
and accounts

02
Helmut Schmid
Otsuka Pharmaceutical 2003
Cover from the annual report
and accounts

03
Commercial Art
*Breaking Barriers Report
and Summary*
Active Communities Network

01

02

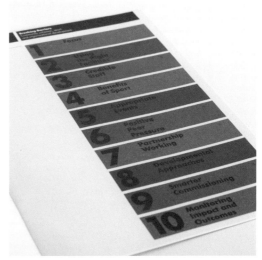

03.
Order

Timetables

Listings

grouwel: a graphic od
useum
3 july 2011

03.1.1
Timetables:
Clarity and simplicity

Image Now undertook the total redesign of the Dublin Bus identity, a project that extended to all route maps and timetables. The approach to the programme was to breathe fresh life into the company's brand, and to consistently represent it in a clear and simple manner.

Every element of the identity was redesigned, from bus livery to street furniture. For route maps and way-finding, clarity and simplicity were enhanced by removing any surplus information and visual clutter. The timetables exemplify this design approach with clear columns for the bus times and large typography for the route numbers.

01
Image Now
Dublin Bus
New identity, route maps
and timetables

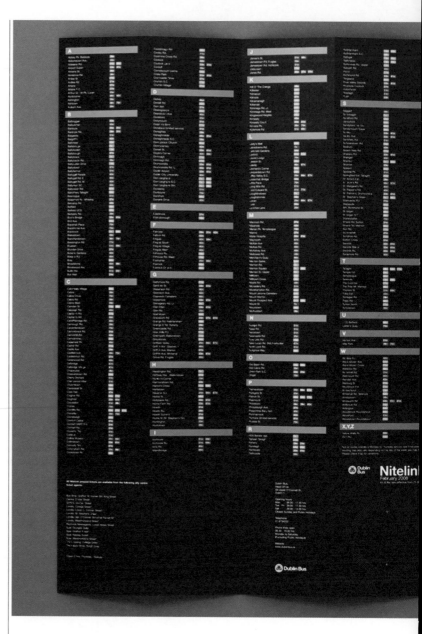

Northbound				Westbound				Southbound			
Route	Monday - Thursday	Friday - Saturday		Route	Monday - Thursday	Friday - Saturday		Route	Monday - Thursday	Friday - Saturday	
27n				25n	No Service			7n			
29n	No Service			39n				15n	No Service		
31n				40n				44n	No Service		
33n	No Service			51n				46n			
41n				66n				48n	No Service		
42n				67n				49n			
				69n	No Service			54n	No Service		
				70n				77n			
				88n	No Service			84n	No Service		

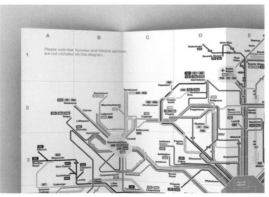

03.1.2
Timetables:
Local durability

A bus system was created especially for the capital of west Iceland, Ísafjörður, and its neighbouring towns with which it shares a bus system using three buses that drive five routes. The brief called for a 'full-size' system that would be taken seriously, but would also reflect the relaxed atmosphere of the towns.

Designs were developed for a map of the area, timetables and additional regional information and were set up at approximately 30 bus stops.

The schedules are changed twice a year (for winter and summer). At each bus stop the timetable features a section of an image from Ísafjörður. To see all the sections that make up the image, travellers must use every stop.

A clean and simple approach was taken for the timetables using a monospace version of the font DIN. Location names run at a 30 degree angle along the top of the timetables, which helps to accommodate the region's sometimes lengthy place names. Each route on the network is given a different colour and small colour swatches are placed under the place names to indicate route intersections.

The identity was designed by Siggi Eggertsson and the metal frames were designed by Stefán Pétur Sólveigarson. The frames were designed and built to withstand the extreme weather the area gets during winter.

01
Atelier Atli Hilmarsson
Public Transport of Ísafjörður
New identity, route maps and timetables

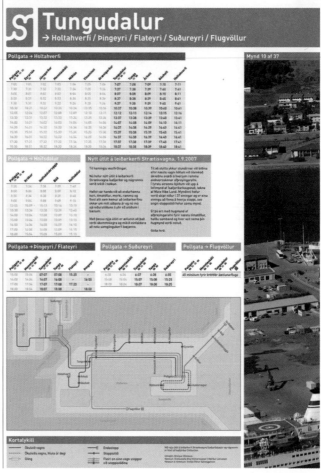

Timetables:
Integrated systems

The Connect Sheffield concept puts
the user at the centre of the design
process, ensuring that information
is carefully planned to be relevant at
each location. Localized street maps
indicating both bus and tram routes
for the city of Sheffield are included
on the signage system. The route
maps and timetables for the bus and
tram network follow the same design
principles and integrate visually with
each other. Shades of grey are used
to provide a neutral background to the
colourful maps.

01
City ID, Atelier Works,
Pearson Lloyd
Connect Sheffield
Wayfinding system

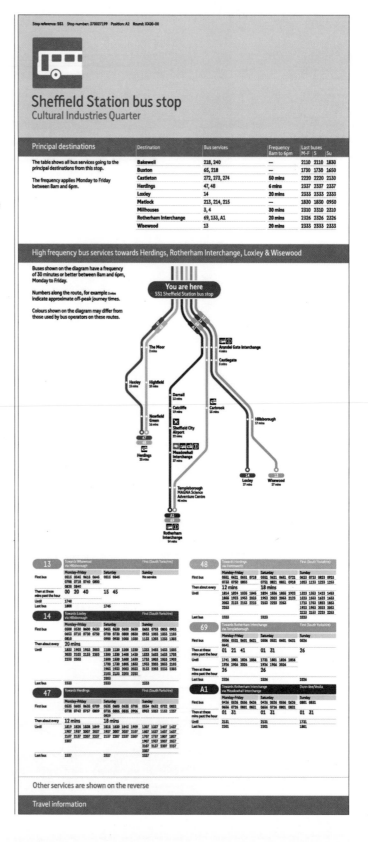

Castle Square Supertram stop
Towards Meadowhall Interchange, Halfway & Herdings Park

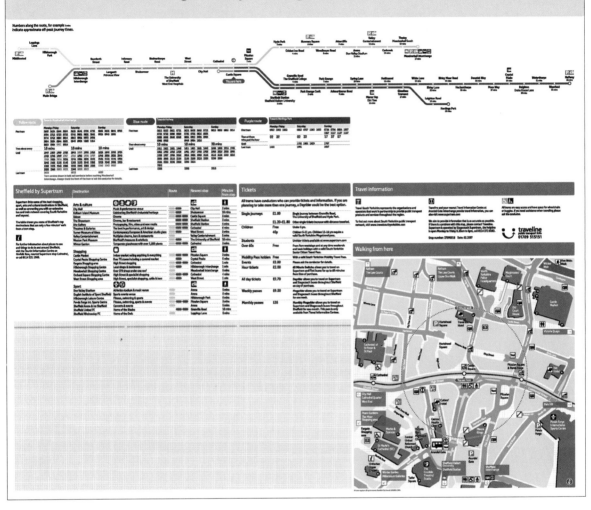

03.1.4
Timetables:
Multiple events

DesignMarch 2009 (HönnunarMars) was the first design festival ever held in Reykjavík.

The visual identity for the four-day festival, which celebrated all aspects of design, is based on two key colours – magenta and cyan – which are overprinted to create purple. The misalignment between the two colours is deliberate and the effect is used on the festival title and on large blocks of colour. The timetable, which is included on the fold-out programme, uses strips of the colours to indicate the various events.

The timetable moves all written information to the left and right margins, allowing the four central panels to become almost abstract as the different strips of colour convey the density of the events. This makes it easy to see the duration of each event and whether it takes place in the morning, afternoon or evening, or over a full day.

01
Atelier Atli Hilmarsson
*HönnunarMars
(DesignMarch 2009)*
Design festival identity
and timetable

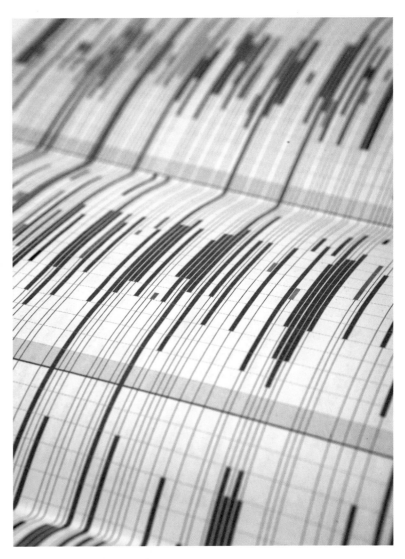

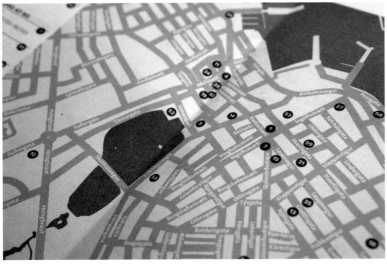

03.1.5
Timetables:
Linear events

To celebrate a major exhibtion by
Dutch graphic design legend Wim
Crouwel at the Design Museum a
set of limited editon posters were
produced by a selection of leading
British design studios. Cartlidge
Levene's poster picks up on the arts
and cultural event listings that were
a large part of the content in Wim
Crouwel's work with Stedelijk Museum
and Van Abbemuseum. The poster
lists the major cultural exhibitions
that were showing in London for
the duration of the Wim Crouwel
exhibition, giving a context to his
show, and forming a kind of calendar
of events for the 96 days the show
ran for.

01
Cartlidge Levene
A Graphic Odyssey Poster
Limited edition silk-screen-
printed poster
Photography: Marcus Ginns

03.1.6
Timetables:
Simplicity and complexity

Simply printed in red on yellow stock, the poster for the spring 2009 lectures at the Sliver Gallery keeps the information clear and simple. All dates are aligned with the months and speakers are stacked up under the months.

24/7 The Alibi is the visualization for an article for the *New York Times Magazine* on a project by the American art professor Hasan Elahi. The image represents his visual alibi for the year 2007 based on data from his Internet site. The publication of his personal details was a reaction to his mistaken inclusion on the FBI's terrorist watch list. The data provides information about Elahi's whereabouts at a particular point in time and the days on which he had a watertight or a leaky alibi are visualized.

01
Paulus M. Dreibholz
Sliver Lecture Series 2009
Events poster

02
Von B und C
24/7 The Alibi 2007
New York Times feature

01

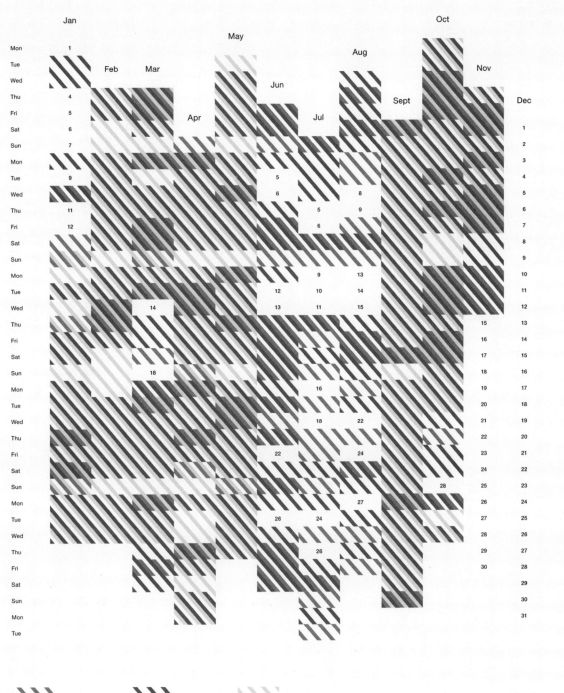

	Jan				May		Aug	Oct		
		Feb	Mar			Jun		Nov	
Mon	1						Sept		
Tue				Apr		Jul			Dec
Wed									
Thu	4								
Fri	5								1
Sat	6								2
Sun	7								3
Mon						5			4
Tue	9				6		8		5
Wed					5		9		6
Thu	11				6				7
Fri	12								8
Sat									9
Sun					9	13			10
Mon					12	10	14		11
Tue			14		13	11	15		12
Wed								15	13
Thu								16	14
Fri								17	15
Sat			18		16			18	16
Sun					18	22		19	17
Mon								20	18
Tue					22	24		21	19
Wed								22	20
Thu							28	23	21
Fri					27			24	22
Sat					26	24		25	23
Sun						27		26	24
Mon						26		27	25
Tue						24		28	26
Wed						26		29	27
Thu								30	28
Fri									29
Sat									30
Sun									31

dated photos of toilets   dated expenses   dated telephone calls

Data source: http://trackingtransience.net

02

One Strip by Ich & Kar is an adhesive wallpaper design that can help children to learn their times tables. There is nothing quirky or strange – just clear and not distracting information.

The series of events leaflets for the *Design Center Stuttgart* by Stapelberg & Fritz features large cropped numbers that indicate the months covered by each leaflet. By cropping the beginning and end of the digits the design suggests an ongoing programme of events of which the leaflet is just a fragment of the whole. Although each design is similar, the numbers are adjusted and cropped differently on each leaflet.

01
Ich & Kar
One Strip
Adhesive wallpaper

02
Stapelberg & Fritz
Design Center Stuttgart
Series of events leaflets

01

03.2.2
Listings:
Dates and times

A series of A5 leaflets and flyers was
designed for Minimum, a menswear
shop and clothing range in Denmark.
Each flyer was purely typographic.
1.440 announced a shopping event
when the menswear shop was open
for a 24-hour period (1,440 minutes).
1.minimum was produced to celebrate
the shop's first anniversary.

A vibrant orange was adopted as the
shop's sale colour. Most shops in
Denmark use yellow for sales, and
in the United Kingdom the colour of
choice is red. For Minimum they were
blended. The 1998 summer sale flyer
plays with the similarity between the
form of the letter S and the numbers
8 and 9.

01
Struktur Design
1.440 minimuminutter
Flyer for a 24-hour shopping
event

02
Struktur Design
1.minimum
Flyer for the shop's first
anniversary

03
Struktur Design
Pre-view
Announcement of two
collection previews

04
Struktur Design
1998 summer sale
Sales flyer

restsalg den 4 juni til 24.00

1.440
minimuminutter

01

02.10.97
02.10.98
1 .minimum

02

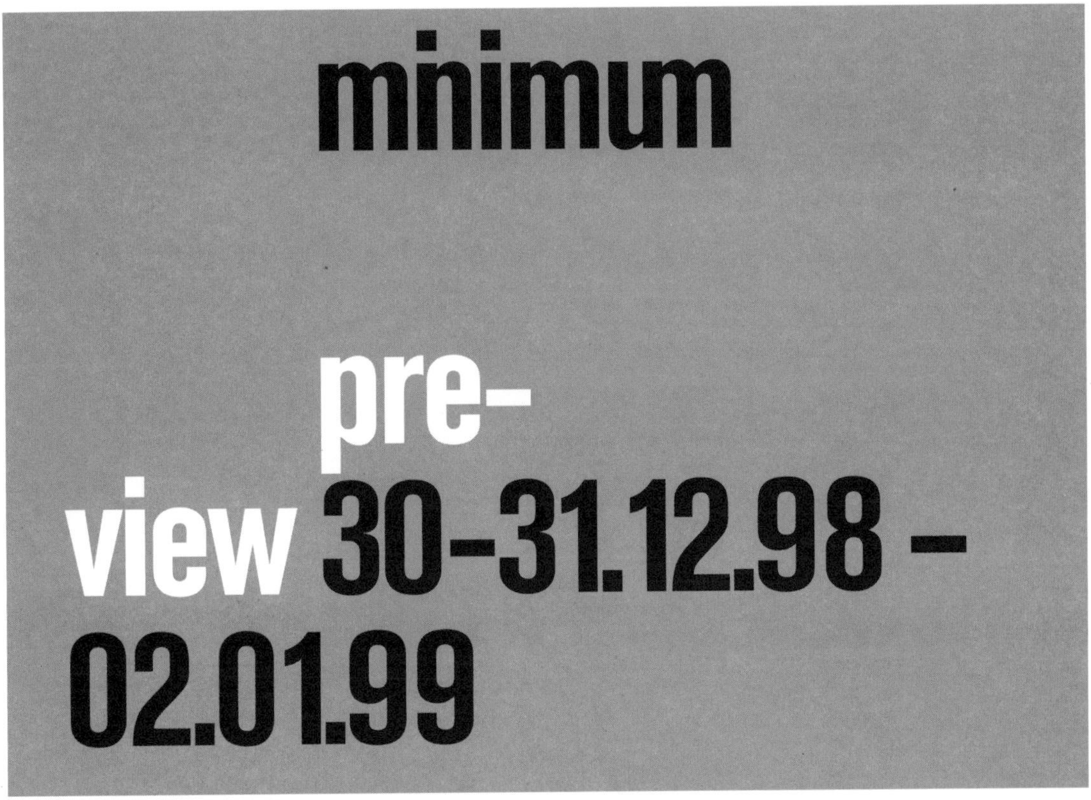

minimum

pre-view **30–31.12.98 – 02.01.99**

1
9
9ummer
8ale

du indbydes
hermed til for-
præmiere på
summer sale
1998

torsdag 25. juni
10.00 – 19.00

fredag 26. juni
10.00 – 19.00

lørdag 27. juni
9.30 – 16.00

minimum

03.2.3
Listings:
Vertical sequences

The vertical format of the two posters designed by Willi Kunz is accentuated by the structure of the information. *Columbia Architecture Planning Preservation* uses long narrow columns that reveal the underlying grid system. The event dates are the most dominant feature of the poster, making up the backbone of its structure, with only discreet mention of the months in which the events take place. By contrast the poster for the Columbia University Graduate School of Architecture and Planning employs greater use of white space. However the bold orange dates are still the key focus of the poster.

01
Willi Kunz
Columbia University Graduate School of Architecture and Planning
Poster

02
Willi Kunz
Columbia Architecture Planning Preservation
Poster

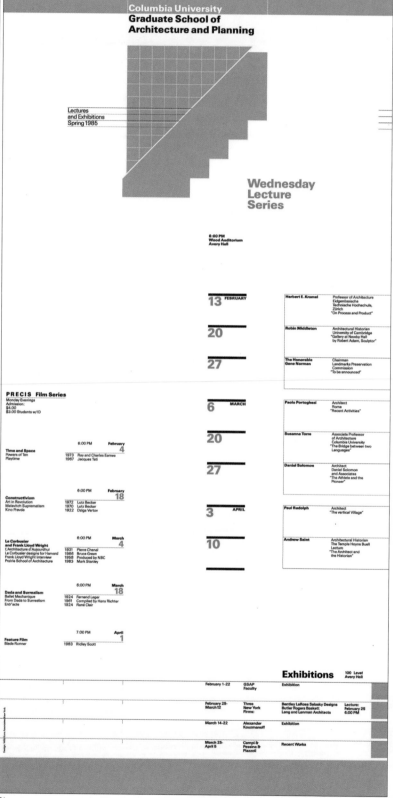

01

Columbia
Architecture
Planning
Preservation

Introduction
Bernard Tschumi, Dean
Mary McLeod
Laurie Hawkinson

**The World Trade Center
and the phenomenon
of 'tallest' towers**
Bill Fischan
Richard Muller
Carol Willis
Paul Byard (moderator)

**Real estate, development,
finance**
Charles Bagli
Richard Plunz
David Stark
Carl Weisbrod
Elliott Sclar (moderator)

**Beyond Finance:
Infrastructure, Ecology,
and Everyday Life**
Petar Arsić
Cynthia Rosenzweig
Andrew Ross
Kathryn Taylor
Sharon Zukin
Stan Allen/Diwon Wright
(moderators)

**Global implications
Trauma and memory**
Mindy Fullilove
Ray Gastil
Andreas Huyssen
Kevin Kennan
Mark Wigley (moderator)

Image and Spectacle
Marshall Berman
Robert Stern
Bernard Tschumi
Joan Ockman (moderator)

Roundtable discussion
Mary McLeod (moderator)

Lectures

6:30pm
Wood Auditorium
Avery Hall

Doors open to
the general public
6:15pm

Spring 2002

February

01
02
WTC Forum

February
28
Ando

Thursday, February 28
1:00pm

Tadao Ando
Architect, Japan

Recent work

March
13
Mori

Wednesday, March 13

Toshiko Mori
Architect, New York
Robert Hubbard Professor
in Practice of Architecture,
Harvard GSD

Material/Immaterial

April
03
Meyers

Wednesday, April 3

Victoria Meyers
Partner,
Hanrahan+Meyers Architects
Adjunct Assistant Professor
of Architecture,
Columbia University

four states of architecture

10
Mendes da Rocha

Wednesday, April 10

Paolo Mendes da Rocha
Architect, São Paulo

Recent work

12
Prouvé

Friday, April 12
4:00–6:00pm

A symposium on the work
of Jean Prouvé in conjunction
with the exhibition
on view in the Arthur Ross
Architecture Gallery

17
Barber

Wednesday, April 17

Benjamin Barber
Professor of Civil Society,
University of Maryland;
Director, New York office
of The Democracy
Collaborative

*Cosmopolitanism vs
Fundamentalism: The City
as Democracy's Forge*

Buell Evening Lecture
co-sponsored by
Skidmore, Owings & Merrill

19
Ito

Friday, April 19

Toyo Ito
Architect, Japan

Recent work

28
Koolhaas

Thursday, February 28
4:00pm

Rem Koolhaas
OMA, Rotterdam
and London

The Lagos Project
Response:
Manthia Diawara, NYU

The Sawyer Seminar,
directed by Andreas Huyssen,
Columbia University

06
Hadid

Wednesday, March 6
6:30pm

Zaha Hadid
Architect, London

Recent work

02
Vidler

Tuesday, April 2
6:30pm

Anthony Vidler
Historian/Theorist

Modernism and Autonomy

Saturday, February 23
10:00am–4:00pm

555 Lerner Hall,
Columbia University

James Marston Fitch Colloquium

Friday, April 12
4:00–6:00pm

A symposium on the work
of Jean Prouvé in conjunction
with the exhibition
on view in the Arthur Ross
Architecture Gallery

Symposia

Exhibitions

January 26–
March 14
**Lucia Stiltanos:
Photography by Candida Höfer**
400 Avery

January 23–
February 15
**Johannesburg:
The Country in the City
Photographs by Jodi Bieber**
100 Avery Hall

February 1–
February 15
WTC Forum
100 Avery Hall

February 18–
March 15
**Havana:
The Photography of Hans Engels**
100 Avery

March 25–
May 10
**Satellite of Love:
Vanishing Beauty of Japanese
Love Hotels**
Curated by Kyoichi Tsuzuki
200 Avery

March 27–
May 3
**Solar:
Photography by Bevan Davies**
400 Avery

March 28–
May 10
**Industrial Alchemy:
Radical Pragmatism in the
Work of Jean Prouvé**
Curated by Evan Douglis
and Robert Rubin
Arthur Ross Gallery, Buell Hall

April 1–
May 3
**Reclaiming the Western
American Landscape**
Curated by Alan Berger
100 Avery

May 18–
June 1
**End of Year
Student Exhibition**
Avery and Buell Hall
Galleries

Target Architecture:
The Role of old Buildings
in the Management
of Global Conflict

sponsored by the
Historic Preservation Program,
Columbia University
Graduate School of Architecture
Planning and Preservation

Friday, April 5
Saturday, April 6

Urban Design:
Practices, Pedagogies,
Premises

Friday, April 5
6:00–9:30pm
Lighthouse International
111 East 59th Street

Shaping Civic and
Public Realms:
What is the Role of
Urban Design?

Saturday, April 6
9:00am–6:00pm
Wood Auditorium
Avery Hall,
Columbia University

Urban Design Practices,
Urban Design Pedagogies
Urban Design Premises

Moderated public discussion
will follow each panel

Sponsored by the
Urban Design Program
Columbia University
Graduate School of Architecture
Planning and Preservation;
Urban Design Program,
Department of Urban Design
and Planning Theory,
GSD, Harvard University;
Van Alen Institute

Design: Inside Out is an A1 poster for lecture forums held at the School of Architecture, Landscape & Design, Leeds Metropolitan University. As it would be displayed on notice boards across the university, it needed to stand out visually among a disparate array of flyers and announcements. Bold, playful typography is used to express the nature of the lecture programme.

For the first in an ongoing set of prints, Mark Bloom of Mash Creative created a series of four themes for the *This Is My Really Useful Poster* series, extending the philosophy and thinking behind his branded *State of the Obvious®* collection. The posters include; *Greenwich Mean Time*, *Emoticon*, *Print Sizes* and *Metric Conversion*.

01
Bibliothèque
Design: Inside Out
Lecture forums poster

02
Mash Creative
This is my Really Useful
Emoticon Poster

03
Mash Creative
This is my Really Useful
Metric Conversion Poster

04
Mash Creative
This is my Really Useful
Greenwich Mean Time Poster

05
Mash Creative
This is my Really Useful
Print Size Poster

Lecture Forums

Leeds Metropolitan University	The Leeds School of Architecture, Landscape & Design	Rose Bowl Lecture Theatre A	Free Entry 18:00 – 20:00 hrs

leedsmet.ac.uk/insideout

2011	13 Jan	3 Feb	17 Feb	3 Mar
	Neil Swanson, Landscape Projects Ltd	Brian Studak, UniversalDesignStudio	Dr Jonathan Chapman, Centre for Research & Development University of Brighton	Andrew Wright, Andrew Wright Associates
	+ Martin Stockley Stockley	+ Jonathon Jeffrey Bibliothèque	+ Trent Jennings Blue Marmalade	+ Tim Ronalds, Tim Ronalds Architects

design: outside

Pecha Kucha Leeds

Leeds Metropolitan University	Students' Union Bar	Free Entry 18:00 – 20:00 hrs	Devised and shared by Klein Dytham Architecture

pecha-kucha.org/night/leeds

2010	28 Oct	18 Nov	2011	20 Jan	20 Feb	20 Mar
	Vol 6	Vol 7		Vol 8	Vol 9	Vol 10

01

02

03

04

05

03.2.5
Listings:
Lines and boxes

Ideas 2007 is an A5 briefing booklet for a creativity conference in the Middle East. The four-day programme of events covered both workshops and conference talks, and a hierarchy of rule weights helps to distinguish between them.

The live music events poster for the Kemia Bar at Momo in London sets out the months and dates in a clear and simple manner. All the information is printed in three languages.

01
Struktur Design
Ideas 2007
Briefing document and programme schedules

02
Ich & Kar
Kemia Bar
Events poster

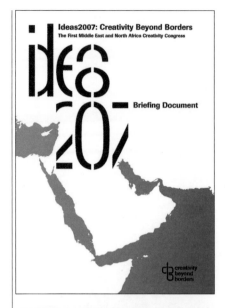

Ideas2007: Creativity Beyond Borders
The First Middle East and North Africa Creativity Congress

ideas 2007

Briefing Document

creativity beyond borders

Outline Programme for the Full Event   23

		Conference	Workshops
6th Friday	Evening	Speakers and delegates arrive	
7th Saturday		Abu Dhabi and Dubai	
	9.30–1.00	Dubai Open Forum: Creativity in the Middle East	
	Evening	Launch of exhibitions: Abu Dhabi and Dubai	
	7.00 pm	Launch of conference: Abu Dhabi	
	7.15 pm	Welcome address: T. Kamali	
	7.30 pm	Buffet dinner and Entertainment: Guests and delegates	
		VIP Dinner: Speakers and special guests	
8th Sunday		Full day conference: Abu Dhabi	
	Morning	Sessions 1 and 2	3 concurrent 3-hour workshops, 1 leader each
	Afternoon	Sessions 3 and 4	3 concurrent 3-hour workshops, 1 leader each
	Evening	Reception, entertainment	
9th Monday		Full day conference: Abu Dhabi	
	Morning	Sessions 5 and 6	3 concurrent 3-hour workshops, 1 leader each
	Afternoon	Sessions 7 and 8	3 concurrent 3-hour workshops, 1 leader each
	Evening	Reception, entertainment	

Programme Schedules

01

january 2002
janfie 2002 **at kemia bar** food every evening from 7 PM till late
valet parking, if you need any further information, please don't hesitate to contact us
0207 434 20 11 / 25 HEDDON STREET - W1 LONDON / momoresto@aol.com
janvier 2002

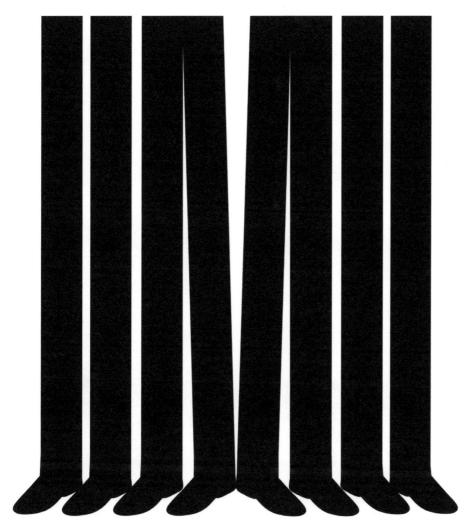

monday, tuesday, wednesday- 21:00	**live music**			thursday, friday, saturday l'khemiss, djemaa, sebte sudi, vendredi, samedi	**momo's music**	
lethnin, thlata, larabaa- 21:00 lundi, mardi, mercredi- 21:00						
	01 tuesday thlata mardi	**02** wednesday larabaa mercredi	**03** thursday l'khemiss jeudi	**04** friday djemaa vendredi	**05** saturday sebte samedi	
	sorry closed	open	resident dj boris	resident dj boris	resident dj boris	
07 monday lethnin lundi	**08** tuesday thlata mardi	**09** wednesday larabaa mercredi	**10** thursday l'khemiss jeudi	**11** friday djemaa vendredi	**12** saturday sebte samedi
roberto pla and his guests salsa	dj simon laurence	**kanda bongo man** congolese soukouse	dj boris	**ray gaskins** jazz funk	guest dj	resident dj boris	resident dj boris	resident dj boris
14 monday lethnin lundi	**15** tuesday thlata mardi	**16** wednesday larabaa mercredi	**17** thursday l'khemiss jeudi	**18** friday djemaa vendredi	**19** saturday sebte samedi
roberto pla and his guests salsa	dj simon laurence	**chartwell dutiro** mbira from zimbabwe	dj boris	**mandisa** soul	guest dj	resident dj boris	resident dj boris	resident dj boris
21 monday lethnin lundi	**22** tuesday thlata mardi	**23** wednesday larabaa mercredi	**24** thursday l'khemiss jeudi	**25** friday djemaa vendredi	**26** saturday sebte samedi
roberto pla and his guests salsa	dj simon laurence	**karuna & sanjeev** urdu and persian poetry	dj boris	**don blackman** funk soul	guest dj	resident dj boris	resident dj boris	resident dj boris
28 monday lethnin lundi	**29** tuesday thlata mardi	**30** wednesday larabaa mercredi	**31** thursday l'khemiss jeudi		
roberto pla and his guests salsa	dj simon laurence	**another fine day** world fusion	dj boris	**lore** trip-hop	guest dj	resident dj boris		

TRUE MUSIC   Budweiser   momo

© ich&kar 2001

03.2.6
Listings:
Super-sized dates

La Casa Encendida is a social, resource and cultural centre in Madrid that hosts a variety of contemporary artistic presentations and educational activities.

The elements that comprise its brochures are a primary colour and five secondary colours for the institution's five departments. The covers of the monthly publications feature a huge date printed in a vibrant green which dominates the cover image.

01
Base Design
La Casa Encendida
Monthly brochure covers

09
11

Cultura
Educación
Para niños y jóvenes
Medio Ambiente
Solidaridad

Jueves01

18.00
Visitas guiadas a la exposición "Inéditos 2011" y atención en sala hasta las 21.00 h

Viernes02

12.00
Visitas guiadas a la exposición "Inéditos 2011" y atención en sala hasta las 14.00 h

18.00
Visitas guiadas a la exposición "Inéditos 2011" y atención en sala hasta las 21.00 h

22.00
Tarde de cuento en la Biblioteca joven
De 6 a 12 años

Sábado03

12.00
Visitas guiadas a la exposición "Inéditos 2011" y atención en sala hasta las 14.00 h

18.00
Visitas guiadas a la exposición "Inéditos 2011" y atención en sala hasta las 21.00 h

La Terraza suena 11
Domingos de julio y agosto
21.00 h
Precio: 4 €
Produce: Bigtimers (http://www.bigtimers.es/)

Llegamos al verano envueltos en celuloide, aunque sea metafóricamente; y es que este año La Terraza quiere reunir a los últimos románticos, artistas que pululan en un universo entre cinematográfico y casi distópico, abocados a discursos sonoros caracterizados en su mayoría por una fragilidad, pasión y personalidad poco comunes, aunque cada uno de ellos fiel a un guión original. Una roadmovie salpicada de personajes entregados de forma incorruptible a un viaje en carretera, conectados a una radio que nos habla de anhelo, deseo y dolor.

Y cuando uno quiere recorrer espacios en los que el horizonte siempre está a más de una canción de distancia, no hay más remedio que volver la mirada a Norteamérica; siete de nueve serán los artistas presentes en La Terraza procedentes del subcontinente americano. Todos ellos nos acompañarán en este fantástico e idealista viaje sonoro.

© Enrique Escorza. La Terraza suena 2010; concierto de Toro Y Moi

Ma06 Inauguración del seminario "Urbanacción". **Mi07** Inicio del Ciclo "Cine indómito. Retrospectiva de Antoni Padrós". **Mi07** Subasta solidaria "Colección Metrópoli". **Sá10** Inicio del Ciclo Artes escénicas y discapacidad 11. **Lu19** Inicio de las proyecciones de **"Todas las cartas. Correspondencias fílmicas".** Mekas, Lacuesta, Rosales, Guerin. **Vi16 Óptica 2011. Festival Internacional de videoarte.** **Mi21 Operación Lem.** Jornadas dedicadas al escritor Stanislaw Lem. **Mi21 En Casa. "No School", de Antonio Ballester.** Inauguración. **Ju22 "Migraciones. Un planeta en movimiento".** Inauguración de la exposición y performance. **Vi23 PoeMaD. Festival de Poesía de Madrid. Ma27** Coloquio con Isaki Lacuesta, So Yong Kim y Jordi Balló. **Mi28 Piensa Madrid 4. La sociedad civil construye.**

Sep

03
10

LA CASA ENCENDIDA

04
10

LA CASA ENCENDIDA

05
10

LA CASA ENCENDIDA

06

LA CASA ENCENDIDA

Verano
en La Casa
Julio y agosto 10

LA CASA ENCENDIDA

Marzo y abril 11

En
Familia

LA CASA ENCENDIDA

**03.2.7
Listings:
*Fragmentation***

The concertina-folded leaflet for
Distribute! 2, a film and video art
event held at the Württembergischer
Kunstverein in Stuttgart, slices up the
bold dates and title. The concertina
folds are staggered so when the
leaflet is closed a section of each of
the panels remains visible. The event's
title fills one side of the folded leaflet
and it is described on the reverse.
As the leaflet is opened, the title
becomes fragmented and the dates
are revealed, together with discreet
information about what will be taking
place during the event.

01
Stapelberg & Fritz
Distribute! 2
Concertina-folded leaflet

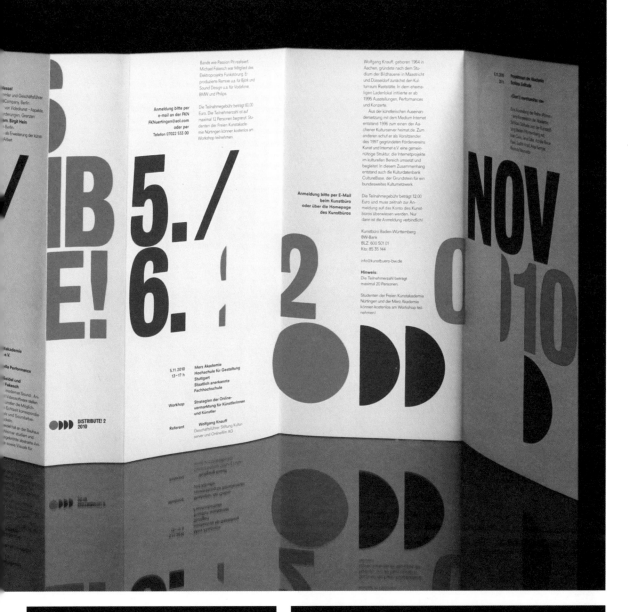

Bands wie Passion Pit realisiert Michael Fakesch war Mitglied des Elektroprojekts Funkstörung. Er produzierte Remixe u.a. für Björk und Sound Design u.a. für Vodafone, BMW und Philips.

Anmeldung bitte per e-mail an der FKN
FKNuertingen@aol.com
oder per
Telefon 07022 533 00

Die Teilnahmegebühr beträgt 60.00 Euro. Die Teilnehmerzahl ist auf maximal 12 Personen begrenzt. Studenten der Freien Kunstakademie Nürtingen können kostenlos am Workshop teilnehmen.

Wolfgang Krauff, geboren 1964 in Aachen, gründete nach dem Studium der Bildhauerei in Maastricht und Düsseldorf zunächst den Kunstraum Raststätte. In dem ehemaligen Ladenlokal initierte er ab 1995 Ausstellungen, Performances und Konzerte.

Aus der künstlerischen Auseinandersetzung mit dem Medium Internet entstand 1996 zum einen der Aachener Kulturserver heimat.de. Zum anderen schuf er als Vorsitzender des 1997 gegründeten Fördervereins Kunst und Internet e.V. eine gemeinnützige Struktur, die Internetprojekte im kulturellen Bereich umsetzt und begleitet in diesem Zusammenhang entstand auch die Kulturdatenbank CultureBase. Der Grundstein für ein bundesweites Kulturnetzwerk.

Anmeldung bitte per E-Mail beim Kunstbüro oder über die Homepage des Kunstbüros

Die Teilnahmegebühr beträgt 12.00 Euro und muss zeitnah zur Anmeldung auf das Konto des Kunstbüros überwiesen werden. Nur dann ist die Anmeldung verbindlich.

Kunstbüro Baden-Württemberg
BW-Bank
BLZ: 600 501 01
Kto: 85 35 144

info@kunstbuero-bw.de

Hinweis:
Die Teilnehmerzahl beträgt maximal 20 Personen.

Studenten der Freien Kunstakademie Nürtingen und der Merz Akademie können kostenlos am Workshop teilnehmen!

5.11.2010   Projektraum der Akademie
20 h   Schloss Solitude

»Don't verhandeln »»

Eva Kusserow der Reihe »Primär-« und Kooperation der Akademie Schloss Solitude und der Kunststiftung Baden-Württemberg mit Inga Clara, Jana Esko, Achille Reese, Freak, Judith Irnaf, Anja Kempe, Manuel Reumuths.

ODDD DISTRIBUTE! 2
2010

5.11.2010   Merz Akademie
13–17 h   Hochschule für Gestaltung
                 Stuttgart
                 Staatlich anerkannte
                 Fachhochschule

Workhop   Strategien der Online-
                 vermarktung für Künstlerinnen
                 und Künstler

Referent   Wolfgang Knauff
                 Geschäftsführer Stiftung Kultur-
                 server und Onlinefilm AG

10	11	12
	01 T 305	
	02 W 306	
	03 T 307	01 T 335
	04 F 308	02 F 336
01 S 274	05 S 309	03 S 337
02 S 275	06 S 310	04 S 338
40 03 M 276	45 07 M 311	49 05 M 339
04 T 277	08 T 312	06 T 340
05 W 278	09 W 313	07 W 341
06 T 279	10 T 314	08 T 342
07 F 280	11 F 315	09 F 343
08 S 281	12 S 316	10 S 344
09 S 282	13 S 317	11 S 345
41 10 M 283	46 14 M 318	50 12 M 346
11 T 284	15 T 319	13 T 347
12 W 285	16 W 320	14 W 248
13 T 286	17 T 321	15 T 349
14 F 287	18 F 322	16 F 350
		17 S 351

04.
Chronology

04.1.1
Calendars:
Dates on film

To commemorate Britain handing over sovereignty of Hong Kong to China in 1997, the designer handcrafted strips of 16mm film, printing letterpress numbers on to them. Twenty-four frames form each day, with each hour charted by a number that increases and decreases in size and weight to form a 'rising' and 'setting' effect. The numbers rise in the west and set in the east until the point of handover on 1 July when power is transferred and the numbers rise in the east and set in the west.

01
Acme Studios
Hong Kong Handover 1997
Letterpress-printed 16mm
film strips

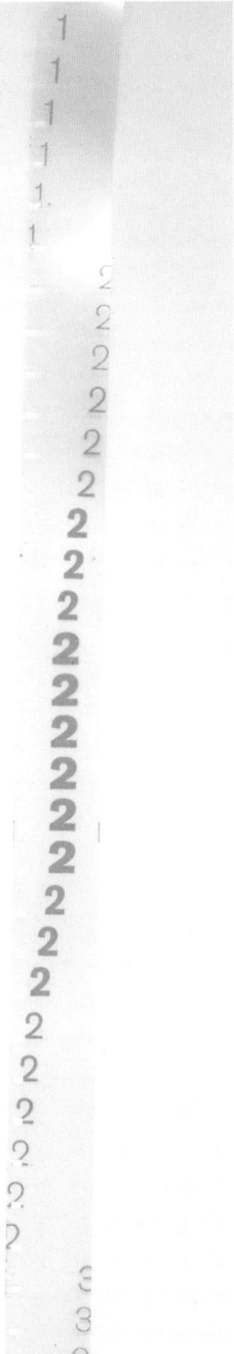

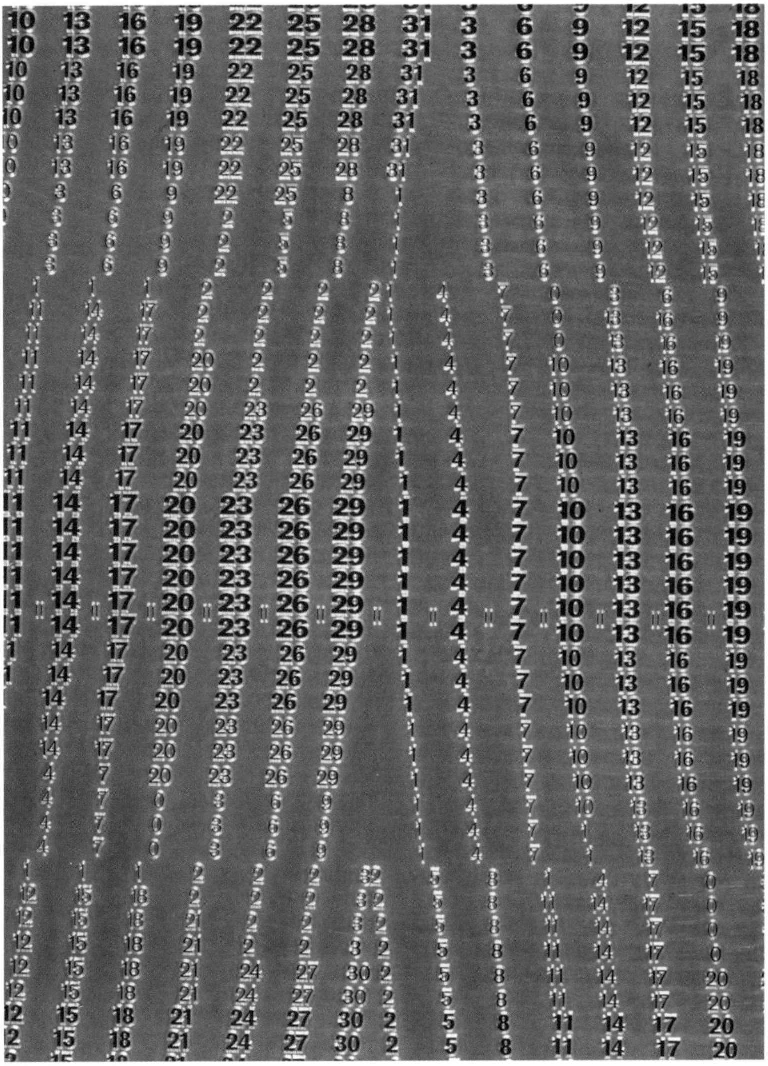

04.1.1
Calendars:
Dates on film

To commemorate Britain's handover of Hong Kong to China in 1997, the designer handmade a Chinese lantern, combining several print processes including silk-screen, rubber stamp and woodblock prints, which were overlaid and printed on both sides of a translucent Chinese paper. The lantern charts both the Gregorian and Chinese calendars of 1997, running from the western world's New Year's Day to the last day of the Chinese New Year in February 1998. Each week is a separate heptagon, hand-built using matchsticks to form the internal structure. The heptagons were then stacked one on top of another, each one shifting sideways a day at a time to follow the position of the moon. The heptagons were then hand-sewn together to form the lantern, which was internally illuminated.

Also shown here are the designer's film strips (see pages 120–121) for the same event. The numbers were letterpress-printed on to 16mm film, projected and then shot on video, and displayed on TV monitors.

02
Acme Studios
Hong Kong Handover 1997
Chinese lantern calendar

03
Acme Studios
Hong Kong Handover 1997
Letterpress-printed 16mm film strips, projected and shot on video

02

03

04.1.2
Calendars:
Targets and blocks

Bullseye is a one-year calendar that covers roughly the training year of 2007 to 2008 in 10m air pistol target practice. Each week is printed on a target used in a recent competition and each target has two shots in it. All the targets are approved by the ISSF (International Shooting Sport Federation). Each target is overprinted in red and black, with the week number large in red at the top and the days of the week running across the centre.

A Post-it style calendar for the Italian company Fedrigoni, a leading supplier of fine papers, has a page per day, a colour per month and perforated fold-up numbers – creating a clever three-dimensional visualization of progress through the year.

01
Hörður Lárusson
Bullseye
10m air pistol
training calendar

02
Studio8 Design
Fedrigoni
Calendar block

01

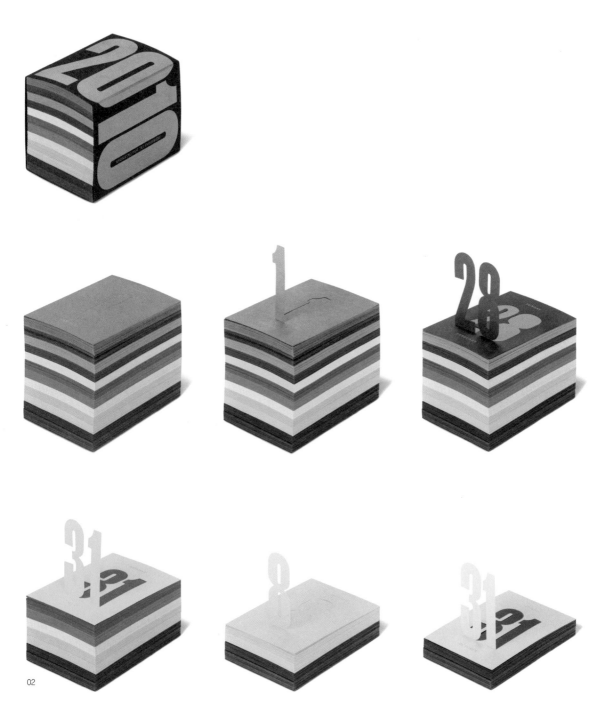

**04.1.3
Calendars:
*Week to view***

A promotional desk calendar (created in two languages) for Fedrigoni displays week-to-view flip-up cards in a colour coordinated sequence. The designers created a custom font for the numbers, which were printed in silver on to various coloured stocks. The calendar creates an original, structural solution to the conventional desk calendar, which relies on the mass of paper to form a stable base.

01
Design Project
Fedrigoni
Desk calendar

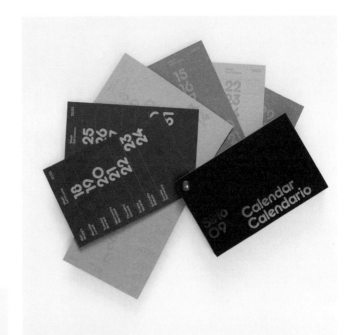

04.1.4
Calendars:
Hundreds and thousands

Seconds is the first in a trilogy of A1 limited edition calendars by Mash Creative. The cut and sliced title text at the top of the calendar is influenced by old analogue flip clocks. Each month is laid out in clean simple columns, which are positioned in a slightly haphazard manner that echoes the look of the title.

Minutes is made up of 525,600 minutes – an average of around 43,800 minutes a month. It is designed to be a typographic representation of the year; each month is broken down into minutes which are listed below each month name. The calendar is printed with glow-in-the-dark ink, which allows the design to look completely different at night. Using the idea of sidereal (star) time, the highlighted months glow like a constellation of stars.

Hours completes teh trilogy, screen printed in black, gold and clear varnish.

01
Mash Creative
Seconds
31,556,926 of them

02, 03
Mash Creative
Minutes
525,600 of them

04
Mash Creative
Hours
8,784 of them

01

02

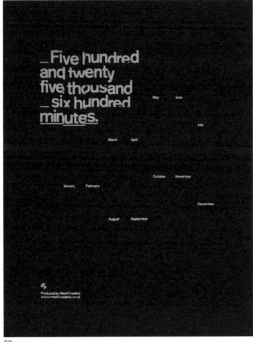

03

04

04.1.5
Calendars:
Order and detail

Struktur Design's 1998 calendar took
the form of an A2 poster printed
in a metallic silver/blue and black.
The days of the week run vertically
down in large white type. These are
followed by 12 columns, one for each
month. All the other text is printed in
black except for weekends, which are
highlighted in white.

The first Struktur Design calendar from
1997, was printed in a muted metallic
gold on to a very thin bible paper,
concertina-folded and sent out in a
clear vacuum-sealed package. The
first panel includes the last month of
1996 and at the bottom of the calendar
a small block showing the start of 1998
bleeds off the sheet.

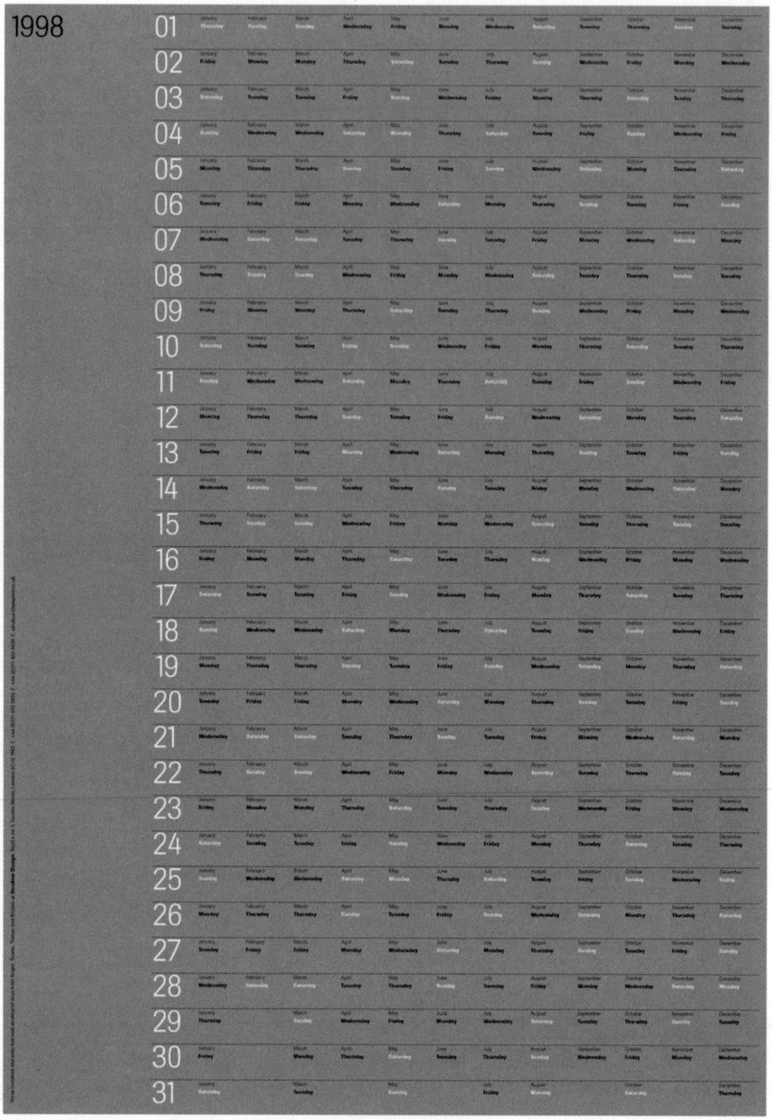

01
Struktur Design
1998 Calendar
A2 poster

02
Struktur Design
1997 Calendar
Concertina folded,
bible paper, measuring
594mm x 210mm

1998

01

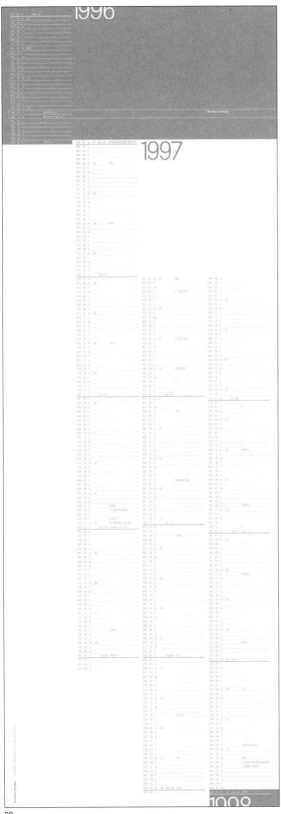

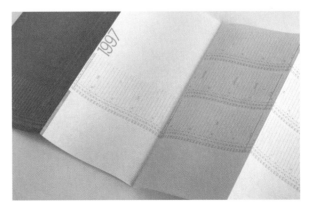

04.1.6
Calendars:
Numerical sequences

The concertina-folded pages of the *Minutes* diary extend to almost 6m in length. The year is broken down into its constituent minutes, all 525,600 of them, printed in fluorescent pink and set at ten-minute intervals. The minutes form a continuous river of numbers over the full length of the diary, punctuated with a return to represent the start of each month. A line space is added along each fold of the diary. This small-scale data is overprinted with the days of the year, 1 to 365 in black. The weeks are highlighted in a warm grey and the months are much larger in a pale tint of the grey. The rhythmic nature of the numerical sequence plays a key role in the appearance of the work.

01
Struktur Design
Minutes
Concertina-folded diary

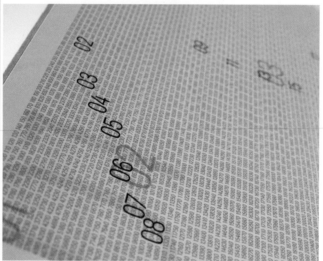

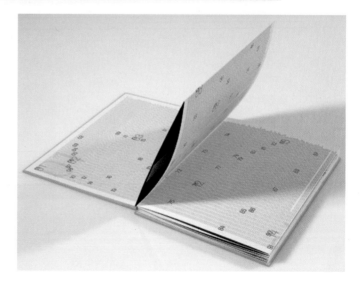

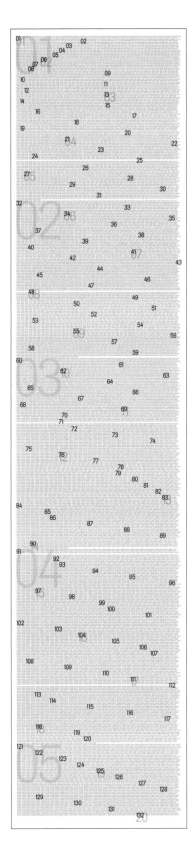
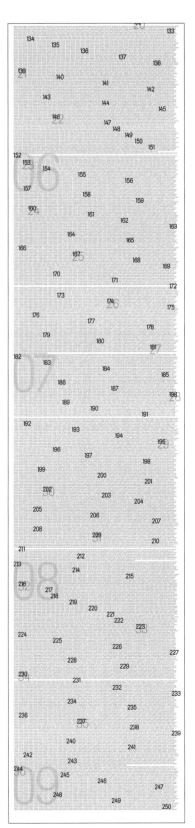
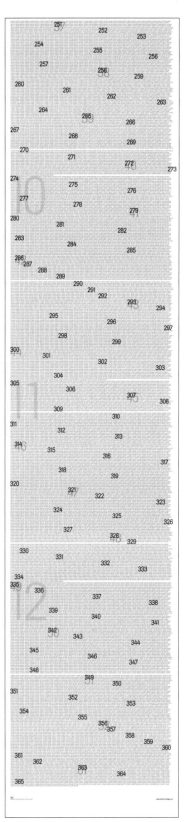

04.1.7
Calendars:
Cut and slice

Working with just two colours,
magenta and a warm yellow, the
designer combined the solid inks to
create a variety of colour combinations
for *31 Days*, a 31-page wall-hung
calendar. The vibrancy of the ink is
further enhanced through the use
of a high-gloss UV varnish which is
applied to each page. Each number
was cut and sliced into a thin strip
as the designer explored the limits
of legibility, resulting in interesting
abstracted typographic forms on
some pages.

52 Weeks, a small 32-page pocket
diary by Struktur Design, features large
cropped slices of the week numbers –
01 to 52. The two digits become wider
and overlap more each week, until by
the end of the year the number has
become an abstracted graphic form.

01
Struktur Design
31 Days
Wall-hung perpetual calendar

02
Struktur Design
52 Weeks
Pocket diary

01

January	January	January	January
01 Monday	08 Monday	15 Monday	22 Monday
02 Tuesday	09 Tuesday	16 Tuesday	23 Tuesday
03 Wednesday	10 Wednesday	17 Wednesday	24 Wednesday
04 Thursday	11 Thursday	18 Thursday	25 Thursday
05 Friday	12 Friday	19 Friday	26 Friday
06 Saturday	13 Saturday	20 Saturday	27 Saturday
07 Sunday	14 Sunday	21 Sunday	28 Sunday

July	July	July	August	August
16 Monday	23 Monday	30 Monday	06 Monday
17 Tuesday	24 Tuesday	31 Tuesday	07 Tuesday
18 Wednesday	25 Wednesday	01 Wednesday	08 Wednesday
19 Thursday	26 Thursday	02 Thursday	09 Thursday
20 Friday	27 Friday	03 Friday	10 Friday
21 Saturday	28 Saturday	04 Saturday	11 Saturday
22 Sunday	29 Sunday	05 Sunday	12 Sunday

November	November	November	November	December
05 Monday	12 Monday	19 Monday	26 Monday
06 Tuesday	13 Tuesday	20 Tuesday	27 Tuesday
07 Wednesday	14 Wednesday	21 Wednesday	28 Wednesday
08 Thursday	15 Thursday	22 Thursday	29 Thursday
09 Friday	16 Friday	23 Friday	30 Friday
10 Saturday	17 Saturday	24 Saturday	01 Saturday
11 Sunday	18 Sunday	25 Sunday	02 Sunday

04.1.8
Calendars:
Multiple choice

Each page of *365* features two perforations which allow the user to separate the pages into three sections. This desk calendar continues Struktur Design's series of calendars where fragments of numbers are combined to create abstract typographic forms. The calendar can be used in a number of different ways and also as a conventional monthly (01 to 12).

365 days of the year format: The left panel represents hundreds, the middle panel tens and the right panel units. The left panel also includes full calendar details at appropriate intervals, together with alternative cuts of the numbers.

Days of the month (01 to 31): This format allows the panel on the left to show a full calendar with dates for a three-month period.

52 weeks of the year: This is similar to the previous format, but uses two large numerals to represent the 52 weeks of the year.

01
Struktur Design
365
Here the desk calendar
is used in a conventional
monthly fashion

02
Struktur Design
365
The calendar can also be
used to show the weeks of
the year 1–52

03
Struktur Design
365
The calendar can also show
the days of the year 1–365

01

02

03

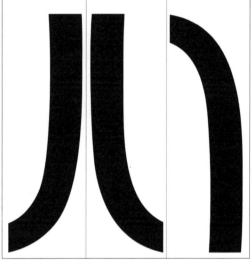

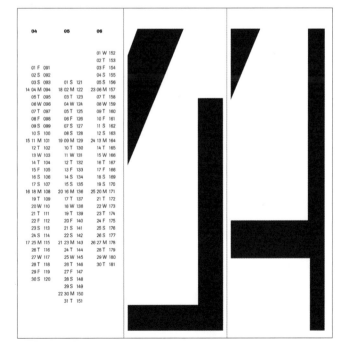

	04	05	06
			01 W 152
			02 T 153
			03 F 154
	01 F 091		04 S 155
	02 S 092		05 S 156
	03 S 093	01 S 121	
14	04 M 094	18 02 M 122	23 06 M 157
	05 T 095	03 T 123	07 T 158
	06 W 096	04 W 124	08 W 159
	07 T 097	05 T 125	09 T 160
	08 F 098	06 F 126	10 F 161
	09 S 099	07 S 127	11 S 162
	10 S 100	08 S 128	12 S 163
15	11 M 101	19 09 M 129	24 13 M 164
	12 T 102	10 T 130	14 T 165
	13 W 103	11 W 131	15 W 166
	14 T 104	12 T 132	16 T 167
	15 F 105	13 F 133	17 F 168
	16 S 106	14 S 134	18 S 169
	17 S 107	15 S 135	19 S 170
16	18 M 108	20 16 M 136	25 20 M 171
	19 W 109	17 T 137	21 T 172
	20 W 110	18 W 138	22 W 173
	21 T 111	19 T 139	23 T 174
	22 F 112	20 F 140	24 F 175
	23 S 113	21 S 141	25 S 176
	24 S 114	22 S 142	26 S 177
17	25 M 115	21 23 M 143	26 27 M 178
	26 T 116	24 T 144	28 T 179
	27 W 117	25 W 145	29 W 180
	28 T 118	26 T 146	30 T 181
	29 F 119	27 F 147	
	30 S 120	28 S 148	
		29 S 149	
		22 30 M 150	
		31 T 151	

04.1.9
Calendars:
Wall planners

A series of annual wall calendars produced by This Studio explores different ways of organizing the year dates. *Two Thousand Eight* represents each month as a simple list of discreet numbers.

Two Thousand and Nine is in a landscape format printed in solid black with white panels left for each day of the week; weekends are in black.

Twenty Ten adopts the look of a conventional year planner with enlarged dates that allow more space for diary entries.

Twenty Eleven reorientates the data: large numbers for each month run across the poster and the days are written as words not as numbers.

Twenty Twelve focuses heavily on the last day of 2011 and the first day of 2012 for the calendar with 31.12.11 and 1.1.12 occupying a large portion of the the poster. The months are organized into three sections, with four months listed in each.

01
This Studio
Two Thousand Eight
Wall calendar

02
This Studio
Two Thousand and Nine
Wall calendar

03
This Studio
Twenty Ten
Wall calendar

04
This Studio
Twenty Eleven
Wall calendar

05
This Studio
Twenty Twelve
Wall calendar

two
thousand
eight
by
this-
studio.
co.uk

01

02

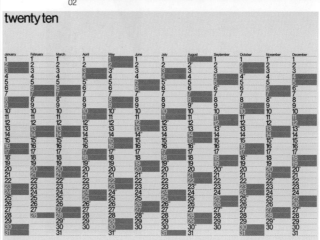

twenty ten

03

04.2.1
Diaries:
Years to view

The exhibition catalogue for the 100th anniversary of the birth of the Swiss playwright and author Max Frisch functions as a 101-year calendar in which personal dates can be entered, but which also highlights key dates in Frisch's work and life. The decades run down each page with key events in his life positioned accordingly. The catalogue produces an interesting and engaging solution that functions successfully as both an informative catalogue/timeline and a usable diary where personal entries rub shoulders with dates that were important to Frisch himself.

01
Eggers + Diaper
Max Frisch 1911–2011
Exhibition catalogue and
diary combined

T : Homo faber | 208 Seiten | P

✳ : 1957

👤 : Walter Faber, Hanna Piper, Elisabeth (Sabeth), [...]
Joachim Hencke

🌐 : Mexiko, Guatemala, New York, Schiff, Frankreich,
Italien, Griechenland, Havanna

📖 : Schicksal/Zufall, Schuld, Technikgläubigkeit,
Versäumnisse, Mythologie, Inzest

! : Flugzeugabsturz, Schlangenbiss in Griechenland

☆ : _____

Sam Shepard in Volker Schlöndorffs Film Homo faber 19[...]

märz

x Schülerzeitung
»Mundus vult
Schundus« kündigt
Stück »Der Schüler
im Himmel« von
MF an

x Walter [...]
nach [...]
der [...]
Wu[...]

✐ Philippe-Film
[Beginn der Au[...]
nahmen für de[...]
[...]

Wer sich nicht mit Politik befasst, hat die politische
Parteinahme, die er sich sparen möchte, bereits
seinbezogen: er dient der herrschenden Partei.

Bertolt Brecht und MF auf die Barcode
Freibad Letzigraben, Zürich 1949

Max Frisch
Eine Ausstellung zum 100. Geburtstag
16.3 – 4.9.2011 im Museum Strauhof, Zürich
Das Begleitbuch zur Ausstellung
www.strauhof.ch

04.2.2
Diaries:
Typographic outlines

Each month of Pentagram's annually updated *Typographic Calendar* is set in a different typeface and, although the months follow the same graphic layout, each one looks very different as a result of the change of font. The cover features the number 365, which is overlaid with the 12 classic and contemporary fonts included set to outline.

Base Design's diary for La Casa Encendida features minimal typography set over pages that have graduated colour blends, from dark to light and back to dark to express the hours of light and dark during the course of the year.

Remake's series of student handbooks and calendars was created for an art and design college in Washington, DC. The handbook for each year features a structured approach to information design coupled with engaging imagery – sometimes typographic, sometimes photographic and sometimes purely graphic. The result is a seamless set of books that present a great deal of varied content in an engaging manner.

01

01
Pentagram
2008 Typographic Calendar
Annually updated calendar

02
Base Design
La Casa Encendida diary
Diary

03
Remake
*Student Handbook
and Calendar*
Cororan College of
Art + Design

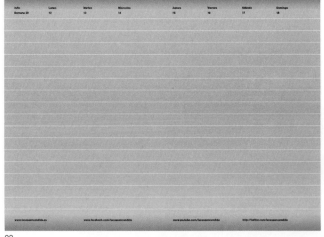

02

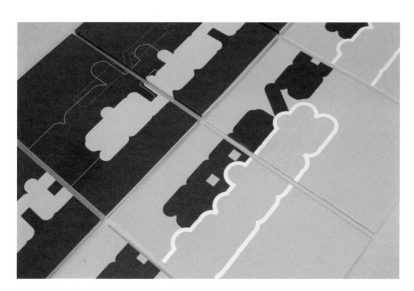

Corcoran College of Art + Design
2003/04 Student Handbook and Student Calendar

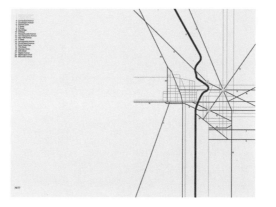

04.2.3
Diaries:
Colour sequences

Each spread of *Hours*, a small A6 diary, represents a month. The left-hand pages illustrate the month with a cumulative total of hours, starting with the first hour on 1 January and continuing to the 8760th hour on 31 December. A different colour is used for the hours in each month, the tint becoming progressively darker for each week of the month. The right-hand pages simply set out the days of the month printed in black; a yellow ink is used for the day of the year and the week of the year. At the end of the diary, pages illustrate the hours during the course of each weekend, and during public holidays.

20 Stationery is a self-initiated boutique stationery brand created by one of SEA Design's founding partners. The clean, classic typography is set against an ever-changing spectrum of background colours that express the change of seasons.

01
Struktur Design
Hours
A6 diary

02
SEA Design
20 Stationery
Desk diary

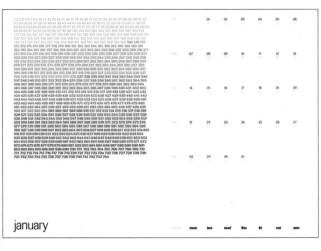

january

july

weekends

01

07
2007

01 Sunday
02 Monday
03 Tuesday
04 Wednesday
05 Thursday
06 Friday
07 Saturday
08 Sunday
09 Monday
10 Tuesday
11 Wednesday
12 Thursday
13 Friday
14 Saturday
15 Sunday
16 Monday
17 Tuesday
18 Wednesday
19 Thursday
20 Friday
21 Saturday
22 Sunday
23 Monday
24 Tuesday
25 Wednesday
26 Thursday
27 Friday
28 Saturday
29 Sunday
30 Monday
31 Tuesday

July
Juli
Juillet
Julio
Juli
Luglio

**04.2.4
Diaries:
*Usability***

In this diary for La Casa Encendida,
fragments of the number 2011 bleed
off the edge of each page, and build
to reveal the full year when the diary
is closed. Large areas of minimal
typography and white space contrast
with the opening spreads for each
month, which are printed full bleed
in vibrant green. Considering that the
diary is printed in only one colour, the
result is one of variety and playfulness.

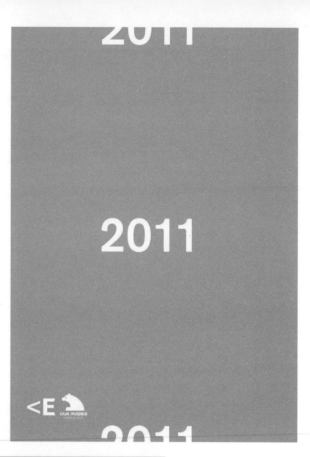

01
Base Design
La Casa Encendida
Diary

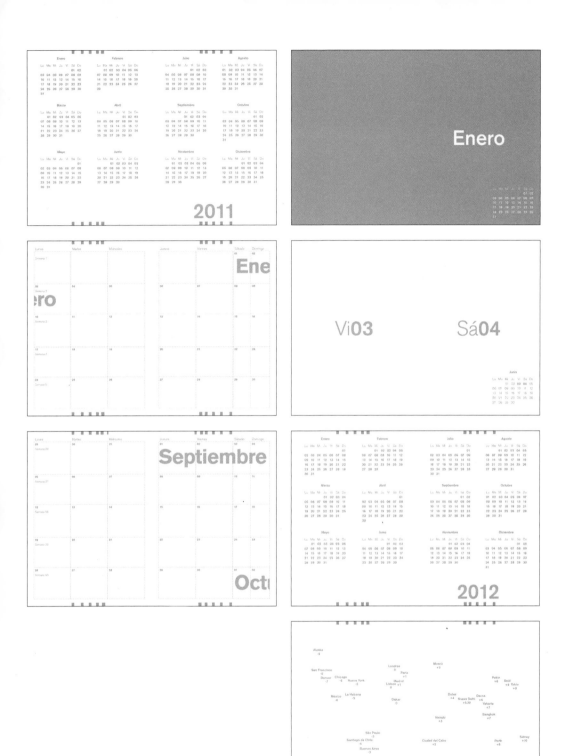

Studio Tonne's *24* is a beautiful
example of the passage of time over a
24-hour period. Starting in the bottom
left corner at 00:00, each minute ticks
past to the right. The angle of the
time refers directly to the angle of the
minute hand on an analogue clock,
so 00:00 reads vertically, 00:15 reads
horizontally and 00:45 reads upside
down. Graceful rhythmic arches are
created through the changing angles
of typography.

Birth Clock is a personal gift to
celebrate the birth of Rosa, at 11:24.

01
Studio Tonne
24
The minute by minute digits
rotate in time with the hands
of a clock

02
Studio Tonne
Birth Clock
A moment forever stuck
in time

01

04.3.2
Clocks:
Digital digits

The *ION* superfamily designed by the Slovakian graphic and type designer Ondrej Jób consists of three families: condensed (ION A), normal (ION B) and wide (ION C). The glyphs are based on the classic seven-segment LCD display. Every ION family has a compelling range of ten weights, and supports more than 70 Latin-based languages and various Open Type features, including discretionary ligatures, fractions and stylistic sets. The family is completed with a special box-drawing font called Cells.

Time:Tone is an audio clock and news feed app for Mute Records. Based around a fascination with measurement, this downloadable toy plays music (from Mute's extensive back catalogue) based on intervals of time: different sounds play on the year, month, day, hour, minute, second, etc. It also automatically downloads news, releases and live event information about Mute's stable of artists.

Malcolm Webb is a personal project from Studio Tonne to celebrate the 40th birthday of Malcolm Webb. Each character is made up of the number 40 laid out in a 10 x 4 grid; the characters are generated by combining black and grey 40s. The 40 years are broken down into weeks, days, hours, minutes and seconds.

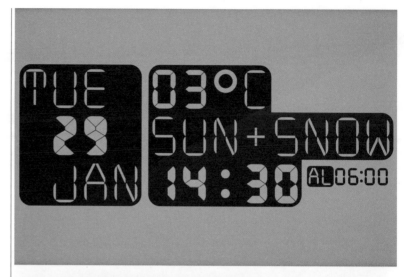

01

01
Ondrej Jób
urtd.net
ION
Typeface design

02
Studio Tonne
Time:Tone
Audio clock and news app
for Mute Records

03
Studio Tonne
Malcolm Webb
40th birthday greeting

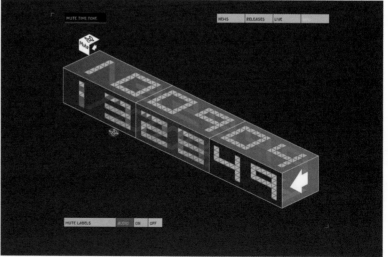

02

MALCOLM WEBB
26 JANUARY 1971 9.45PM

HAPPY BIRTHDAY
FROM THE FARRINGTONS

04.3.3
Calendars:
Atomic clocks

Studio Tonne were commissioned to design an article for Audi's customer magazine. This issue of the magazine had a 24-hours theme, and *How Long are 24 Hours Anyway?* provides a view of how the 230 atomic clocks around the world synchronize, connecting to clocks and computer networks using radio signals.

One second is defined as 9,192,631,770 vibrations of a caesium-133 atom. Scientists measure the fluctuations of a single electron around the nucleus. There are 55 electrons in total – 54 around the nucleus, and a single one in 'orbit' around the others.

01
Studio Tonne
How Long are 24 Hours Anyway?
Audi magazine

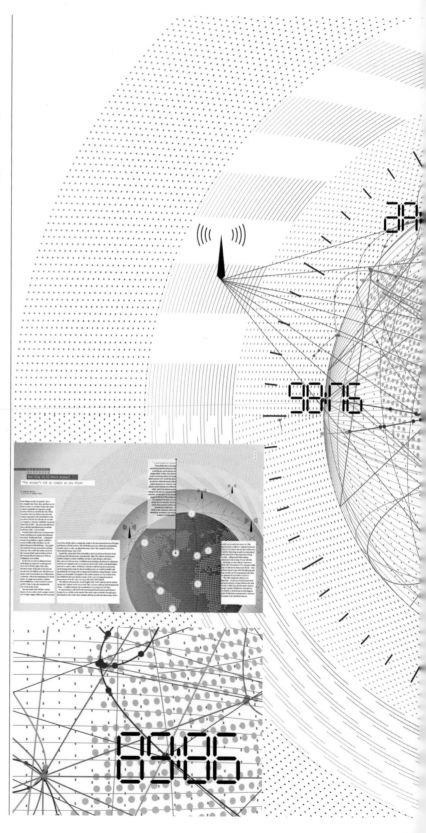

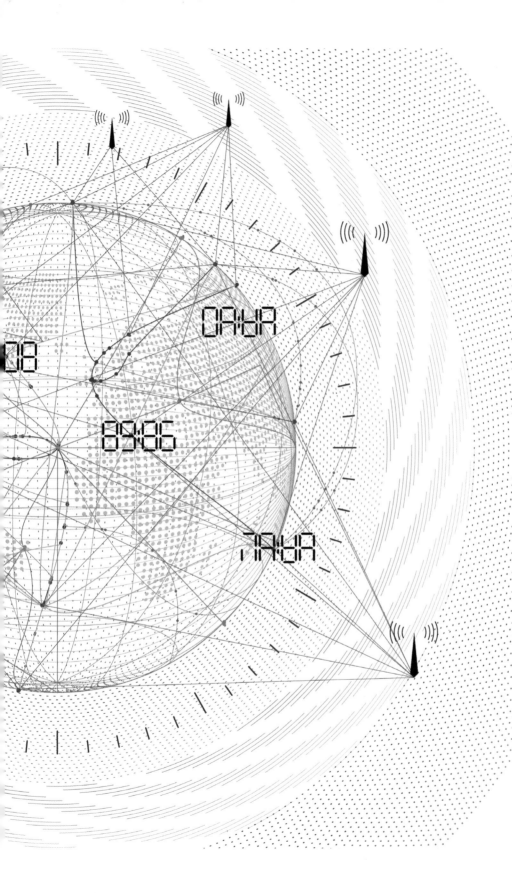

04.3.4
Clocks:
Clock apps

TimeDevice 01 is an iPhone app produced in a collaboration between Chilli X and the type designer Rian Hughes. The hour and minutes are displayed in a bold black font while the seconds display darkens slowly over the course of a minute. The background colour can be left to change automatically, in which case it fades slowly through the spectrum, or manually – the phone is shaken to select a random colour.

NightTime Plus is an iPhone alarm clock inspired by traditional LCD displays. The display can be customized with different colours and textures.

AboutTime tells 'about what time it is' and features beautifully rendered typography on a light parchment background. It is bright during the day and dark at night. It makes an ideal (and unusual) bedside clock. As well as telling the time in a unique and unconventional way, its pages can also be flipped to reveal entertaining quotes and musings on the nature of time itself.

F-Clock is a split-flap clock that mixes an analogue concept with a digital spin. *U-Clock* visualizes time as a series of bars which move across the screen.

01, 02
Chilli X and Rian Hughes
TimeDevice 01
iPhone clock

03
Chilli X
NightTime
iPhone clock

04
Chilli X
NightTime Plus
iPhone clock

05, 06
Chilli X
AboutTime
iPhone clock

07, 08
Winfield & Co.
F-Clock
iPhone clock

09, 10, 11
Winfield & Co.
U-Clock
iPhone clock

01

02

03

04

05

06

07

08

09

10

11

04.3.4
Clocks:
Clock apps

TextClock, Commune Inc.'s iPhone app, treats the time as a sequence of words – there are no numbers.

ClickClock is based on the circular motion of an analogue clock. The minutes and seconds orbit the hour which is positioned in the centre of the screen.

WordClock is a typographic clock and interactive artwork for Mac, iPad and iPhone. Time is shown by highlighting appropriate words from one of over 30 languages. Users can select either the linear or dynamic rotary version, or periodically transition between the two.

12

12
Commune Inc.
TextClock
iPhone clock

13
Coffeecoding
ClickClock
iPhone clock

14
Simon Heys
WordClock
Screen saver for Macs,
iPads and iPhones

13

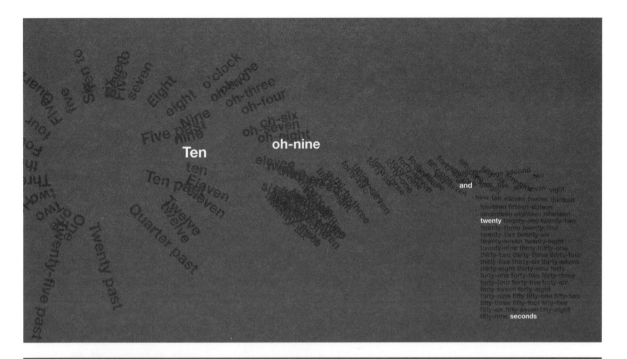

Five past Ten past Quarter past Twenty past **Twenty-five past** Half past Twenty-five to Twenty to Quarter to Ten to Five to One one Two two Three three Four four Five five Six **six** Seven seven Eight eight Nine nine Ten ten Eleven eleven Twelve twelve o'clock oh-one oh-two oh-three oh-four oh-six oh-seven oh-eight oh-nine eleven twelve thirteen fourteen sixteen seventeen eighteen nineteen twenty-one twenty-two twenty-three twenty-four twenty-six twenty-seven twenty-eight twenty-nine thirty-one thirty-two thirty-three thirty-four thirty-six thirty-seven thirty-eight thirty-nine forty-one forty-two forty-three forty-four forty-six forty-seven forty-eight forty-nine fifty-one fifty-two fifty-three fifty-four fifty-six fifty-seven fifty-eight fifty-nine **and** precisely one second two three four five six seven eight nine ten eleven twelve thirteen fourteen fifteen sixteen seventeen eighteen nineteen twenty twenty-one twenty-two twenty-three twenty-four twenty-five twenty-six twenty-seven twenty-eight twenty-nine thirty **thirty-one** thirty-two thirty-three thirty-four thirty-five thirty-six thirty-seven thirty-eight thirty-nine forty forty-one forty-two forty-three forty-four forty-five forty-six forty-seven forty-eight forty-nine fifty fifty-one fifty-two fifty-three fifty-four fifty-five fifty-six fifty-seven fifty-eight fifty-nine **seconds**

Ten past ten and ten seconds

04.3.5
Clocks:
Explorations in time

SEA Design contributed a series of proposals for an updated watch interface to *ICON* magazine. The designs represent a rethinking of the digital watch for the twenty-first century, free from the limitations of traditional LCD displays.

Farrow Design were comissioned by the contemporary furniture company SCP to produce a series of wall clocks. *Notime*, *Nightime* and *Finetime* are based on conventional analogue clocks but feature clean, refined graphics to give a fresh contemporary look.

01
SEA Design
Icon Watches
Watch concept designs

02
Farrow Design
Notime
SCP wall clock

03
Farrow Design
Nightime
SCP wall clock

04
Farrow Design
Finetime
SCP wall clock

01

02

03

04

04.3.6
Clocks:
Organizing time

For *Struktured Clock*, Struktur Design reorganized and rationalized a conventional analogue clock. Based on a 24-hour clock, the hours and minutes are in columns on either edge of the square clock face.

Twenty Four Hour Clock was produced as a result of an open brief set by London-based specialist printers Artomatic. The A2 silk-screen-printed poster was designed as part of an ongoing research project looking at time systems, and works as a direct extension of the Struktur Design calendars and diaries (see pages 130–137, 144). The poster sets out every second, minute and hour of a 24-hour period, with each time-measuring unit reproduced in a progressively larger point size.

01

01
Struktur Design
Struktured Clock
Analogue clock

02
Struktur Design
Twenty Four Hour Clock
A2 limited edition poster

twentyfour hour clock
design by abstract. printed by antoinette.

05.
Abstraction

05.1.1
Deformation:
Three-dimensional forms

The flyer for entries to the Focus
Open 2011 international design awards
features large three-dimensional
characters that give it a sense of
space. The numbers for the year
2011 are haphazardly placed within
the space alongside the word 'open'.
The zero letter form is interchangable
with the O of 'open'. The book cover
populates these three dimensional
forms with various featured products
from within the annual, transforming
the letters into pieces of furniture.

The *Firestation Workshops 2004*
poster, an artists' studio complex in
Dublin, uses a stencil typeface for the
tiling, which is fragmented across the
page. The numerals 2004, printed in
red, contrast with the scale of the
tiles, while the zeros echo the form
of the sculpture in the bottom right
of the poster.

01
Stapelberg & Fritz
Focus Open 2011
Baden-Württemberg
International design
awards flyer

02
Stapelberg & Fritz
Focus Open 2011
Baden-Württemberg
International design awards
Annual book cover

03
Atelier David Smith
Firestation Workshops 2004
Workshop programme poster

01

02

WORKSHOPS 2014

FIRESTATION

John Carrick / Rita Duffy / Noel Kelly / David Kinnane / Caroline Madden / Deirdre McLoughlin / Tanya Elliot Nyegaard / Geraldine O'Neill / Niall O'Neill / Alan Phelan

The annual artists' workshop programme offers exciting, challenging and innovative opportunities for the career development of visual artists

Fire Station Artists' Studios, 9/11 Buckingham Street, Dublin 1. Telephone: 01 855 6735. Fax: 01 855 5632

www.firestation.ie

05.1.2
Deformation:
Numbers from nothing

Self-initiated posters by Pentagram, *The Number Series* explores the boundaries of legibility. Stylistically each poster is very different from the next; however, the series is held together by the consistent use of black with glimpses of other colours just visible.

01
Pentagram
The Number Series
Posters 0–5

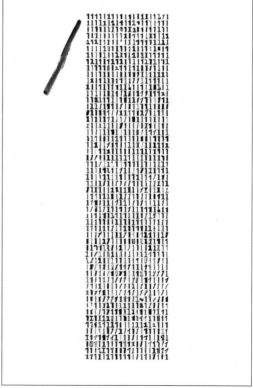

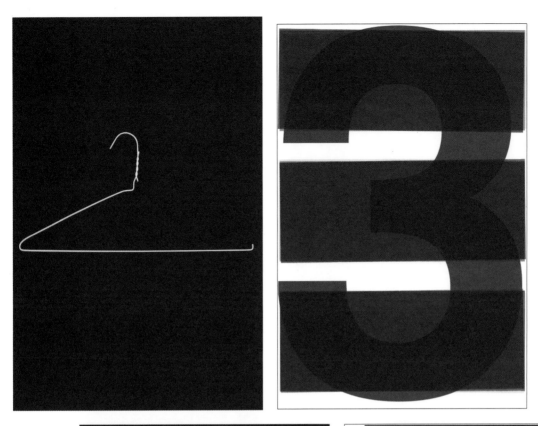
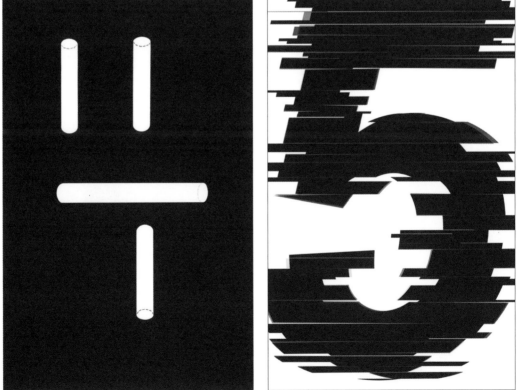

05.1.2
Deformation:
Numbers from nothing

These posters from *The Number Series* by Pentagram explore the use of negative space; the six is simply formed from a rectangle and a square. The seven features two white triangles on a grey background, the eight crops in to two elipses and the nine is two cresents and a circle.

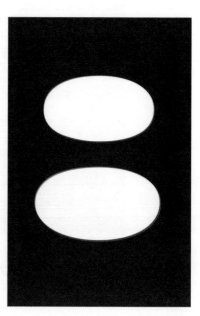

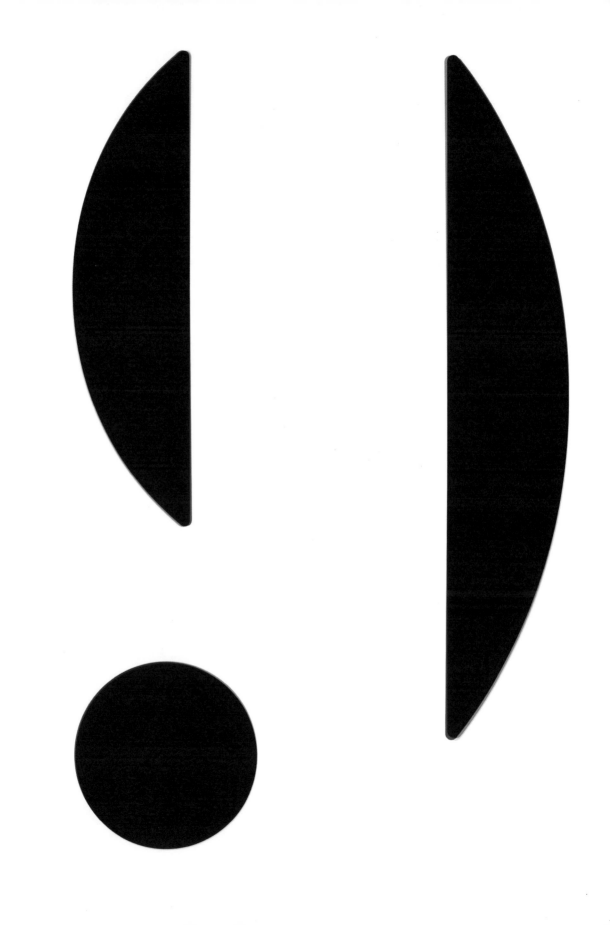

05.1.3
Deformation:
Freehand

Minnie's 8th Birthday is an invitation to the designer's daughter's eighth birthday party at a local ice rink. Minnie drew the figure 8 with different coloured LED lights.

Bunch Design's promotional material for 55DSL, a fashion brand from Diesel, treats the numbers 55 and 555 in a hand-drawn graphic manner. The *55DSL Tote Bag* features the number 55 constructed out of interlaced hand-drawn tubes and printed in the company's corporate colours of red, white and blue.

The *555 poster* is based on a Christmas in-store campaign '55DSL Has Your Christmas All Taped Up'. For this staff were encouraged to apply specially printed green branded packing tape to almost any inanimate object in-store, and the poster continues this theme by wrapping the three 5s in green tape.

01
Struktur Design
Minnie's 8th Birthday
A birthday invitation drawn with light

02
Bunch Design
55DSL Tote Bag
Limited edition screen-printed bag

03
Bunch Design
555 Poster
55DSL Christmas in-store incentive campaign

Minnie's 8th birthday party on Ice*
Saturday 7th June
2.30—4.00pm

*

At the Sobell Leisure Centre,
Hornsey Road, N7

Don't forget to wrap up warm
(gloves and thick socks)

Parents are welcome to have a
go and if your child hasn't been
before it could be useful to give
them a hand!

RSVP
Sanne on 07725 55 20 20
sanneft@mac.com

01

02

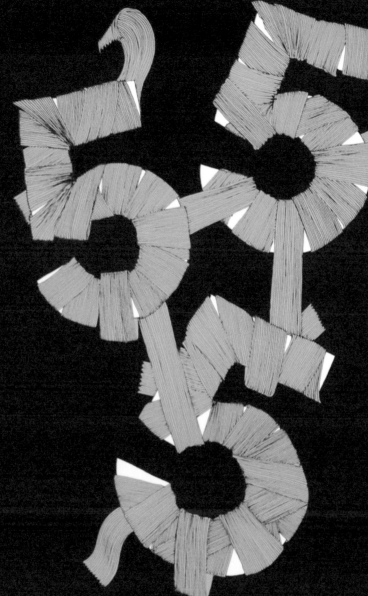

**55DSL HAS
YOUR CHRISTMAS
TAPED UP**

05.1.4
Deformation:
Circles and lines

GP is 10 is a dual-purpose, limited edition brochure for printers Generation Press that celebrates their tenth anniversary and also showcases their print prowess and techniques to new and existing clients. The cover features the title overprinted in cyan, magenta and yellow with the number 10 repeated in black. Inside, a series of folded sheets showcases a variety of print processes. Included is an interesting numeric type design constructed predominantly from circular elements.

01
Build
GP is 10
Brochure

05.1.5
Deformation:
Illustration by numbers

The children's book *Bugs by the
Numbers* is a playful and educational
resource full of bug facts and figures.
Each spread focuses on a different
insect, which is illustrated entirely from
numbers in different weights, sizes
and fonts. The book also includes
die cuts and flaps to further intrigue
young readers.

01
Werner Design Werks
Bugs by the Numbers
Children's book

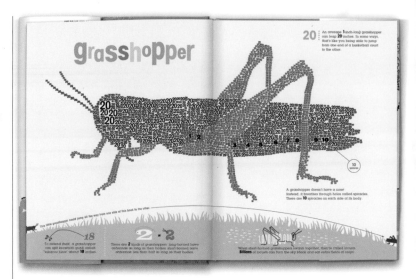

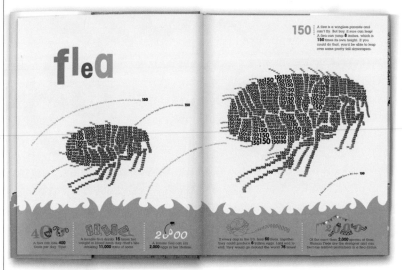

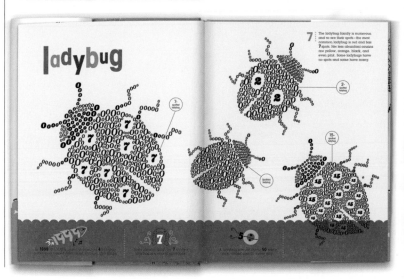

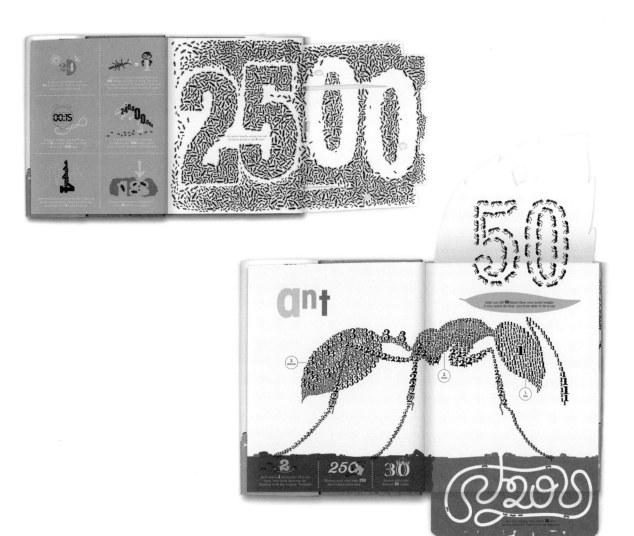

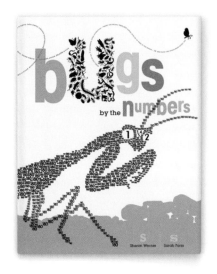

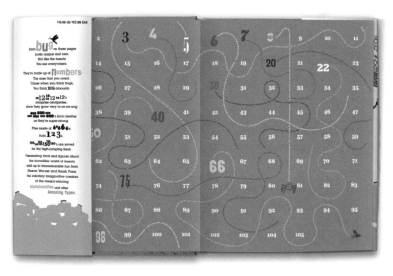

05.1.6
Deformation:
Type as image

For eight consecutive years Werner Design Werks produced *WDW Number Glasses*, a series of cocktail glasses that were given to friends, clients and suppliers. Each year had a different number and a different cocktail recipe. The idea: keep it simple, make it functional and be sure the recipes taste good. The quirky selection of fonts built into an interesting typographic mixture over the years.

Each month of the typographic desk calendar produced for Consultants Group by Bunch Design is illustrated typographically through numbers, for example swan heart 2s for February and ice cream 7s for July.

'Erotipo', the erotic side of typography, was the theme of a course held at the Iuav University of Venice by Leonardo Sonnoli. The course was the result of research by Sonnoli and Irene Bacchi into the relationship between type, typography and the human body. Featured here are examples by Sonnoli from the eighth issue of the weekly publication *FF X-TRA*, which combine various numbers with human forms.

01
Werner Design Werks
WDW Number Glasses
Promotional cocktail glasses

02
Bunch Design
Typographic Desk Calendar
Promotional calendar for
Consultants Group

03
Leonardo Sonnoli
FF X-TRA
Erotic typography
experiments

01

02

03

05.2.1
Vernacular:
Lost and found

Leonardo Sonnoli collaborated with Sara Fanelli and George Hardie on designs for a series of numbers for the fourth annual *If You Could Collaborate* exhibition, a self-initiated project by London-based art directors Will Hudson and Alex Bec.

Contributors to the exhibition were asked to produce something unexpected, by working with a partner from any discipline, profession or background. There was no brief to answer or format to honour. The exhibition presented works produced by 33 teams at the A Foundation Gallery, Rochelle School in London. The exhibits ranged from classic framed pieces to more ambitious, experimental sculptures, films and installations.

The series of numbers ranges from hand-drawn doodles to elements of found vernacular lettering.

01
Leonardo Sonnoli, Sara Fanelli, George Hardie
If You Could Collaborate
A collaboration in counting

GEORGE HARDIE &
LEONARDO SONNOLI &
SARA FANELLI

In 2003 Leonardo Sonnoli took George Hardie shopping in his hometown, Rimini. They discovered an ancient stationer's shop, with a box of huge rubber stamps in the window. George asked Leonardo if he could enquire whether the owner had the matching letters. The proprietor explained, apologetically, that because there are 26 letters in the alphabet, he had never felt that he could afford to stock letters. He had stuck to NUMBERS, which were

On the same day George and Leonardo bought some vintage EXERCISE books for Sara Fanelli.

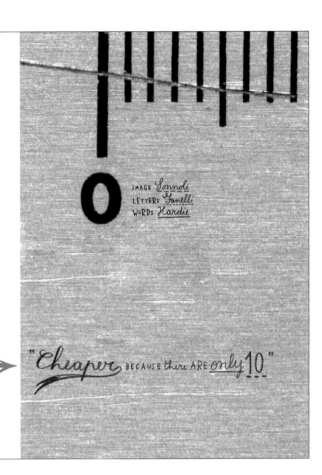

IMAGE Sonnoli
LETTERS Fanelli
WORDS Hardie

"Cheaper BECAUSE there ARE only 10"

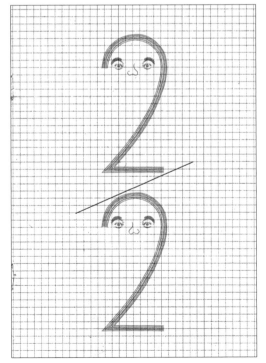

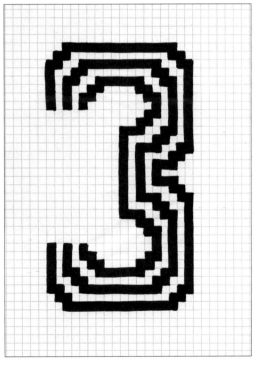

More examples from Leonardo
Sonnoli's collaborative series
If You Could Collaborate.

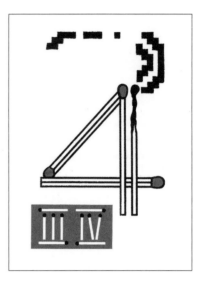

02
Leonardo Sonnoli, Sara
Fanelli, George Hardie
If You Could Collaborate
A collaboration in counting

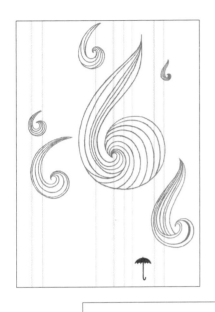

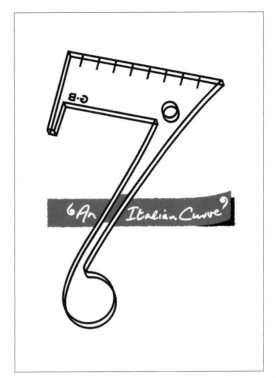

"An Italian Curve"

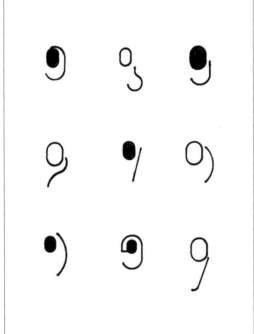

05.2.2
Vernacular:
Graphic elements

The *Phil Harrison Award* is a one-off, custom-made presentation piece, commissioned by Sony Computer Entertainment Europe (SCEE) to present to the president of SCE worldwide when he left the corporation. The design celebrates his 15 years as a key figure in the development of Sony Playstation consoles. The award is screen-printed on six layers of plexiglass, encased in an acrylic box frame. Graphic elements of the evolution of the Playstation console are combined to form the number 15.

01
Build Design
Phil Harrison Award
Commissioned by Sony
Computer Entertainment
Europe (SCEE)

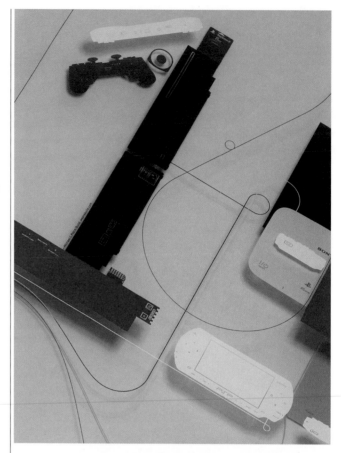

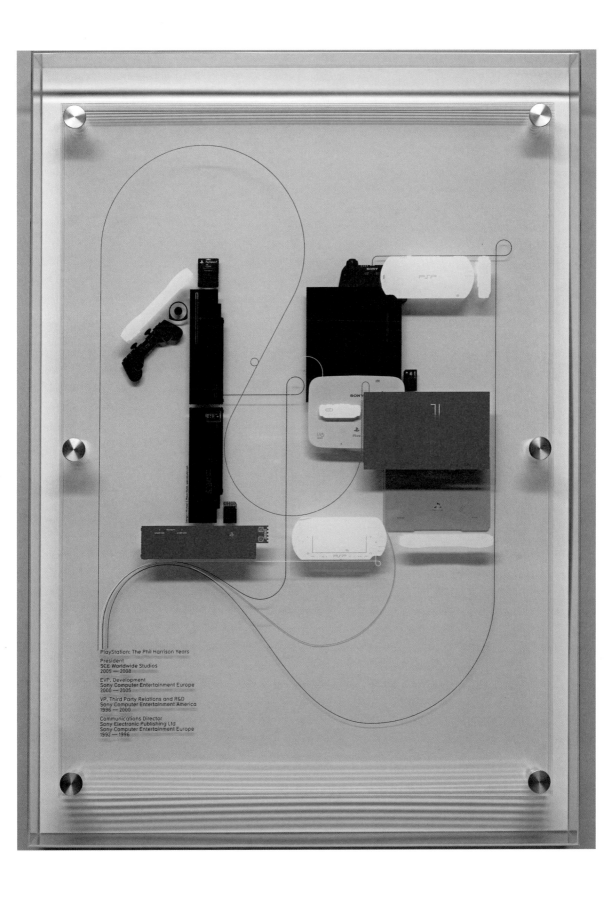

PlayStation: The Phil Harrison Years

President
SCE Worldwide Studios
2005 — 2008

EVP, Development
Sony Computer Entertainment Europe
2000 — 2005

VP, Third Party Relations and R&D
Sony Computer Entertainment America
1996 — 2000

Communications Director
Sony Electronic Publishing Ltd
Sony Computer Entertainment Europe
1992 — 1996

05.2.3
Vernacular:
Numbers in space

SEA Design worked alongside
the contemporary office furniture
manufacturer Ahrend to create
promotional literature for the *Four_Two*
range of work, bench, meeting and
conference tables. The art-directed
images not only illustrate the flexibility
of the furniture system but are also
cleverly set up to form the numbers
4 and 2.

01
SEA Design
Ahrend Four_Two
Promotional material

05.2.4
Vernacular:
Scratch and burn

Pentagram's poster for the film *26 - Fifty Years In Prison* combines an elegant minimal design with the large red number 26, which is offset against the rough scratched marks made to count the 50 years spent in prison.

Painstakingly constructed from matchsticks, *15 One Two*, the opening image for an article in *Wired* magazine, gives a sense of structural space to the letter forms, just before they burn to the ground.

01
Pentagram
26
Promotional movie poster.

02
Doyle Partners
15 One Two
Illustration for *Wired* magazine

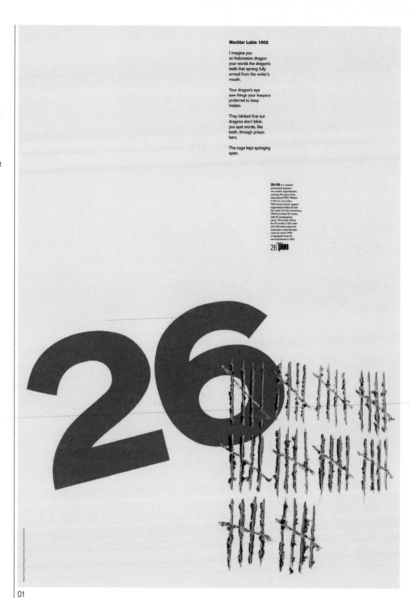

01

05.2.5
Vernacular:
Numbers everywhere

The American architecture and design magazine *Metropolis* celebrated its 30th anniversary with a specially commissioned cover designed by Doyle Partners. The cover image is constructed from a large sheet of card that is folded in such a way as to form the number 30. Issue dates are printed along the entire edge of the construction.

Exquisite Clock is a research project developed in 2008 at Fabrica by the Brazilian grantholder. *Exquisite Clock* is made of numbers taken from everyday life – seen, captured and uploaded by people all over the world. Built around an online database, the clock exists as a Web 2.0 website, an iPhone application and a series of site-specific installations.

01
Doyle Partners
30 Years Anniversary Cover
Metropolis magazine

02
Fabrica/Joao Wilbert
Exquisite Clock
An interactive installation,
web- and app-based clock.
Installation view from
*Decode: Digital Design
Sensations* at the Victoria
& Albert Museum, London

03
Fabrica/Joao Wilbert
Oriol Ferrer Mesia
Exquisite Clock
An interactive installation,
web- and app-based clock.
Installation detail

04
Fabrica/Joao Wilbert
Exquisite Clock
An interactive installation,
web- and app-based clock,
images from the website

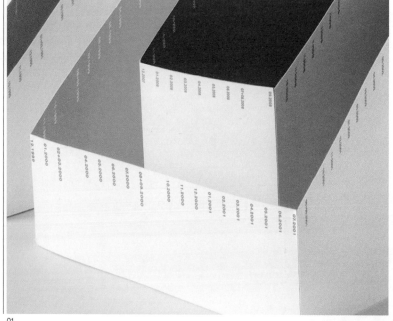

01

02

03

04

05.2.6
Vernacular:
Contemporary and classic

Bunch Design incorporated the New York dialling code 212 into the logo for *1212NYC*, a photography exhibition by Mario Delic. For the B1 fold-out invitation/poster the designers splashed the logo across one side; the other side displayed one of Delic's photographs. The typography of the logo has a distressed and decaying quality that reflects the style of photography in the exhibition.

Printed on a heavy black card, *Eurotower 2* is an invitation to celebrate the second anniversary of the Zagreb skyscraper, Eurotower. It features white foil embossing, and a number 2 based on the tower's signature windows. The company's logo is clean, modern and linear, but the design creates a classical serif 2.

01
Bunch Design
1212NYC
B1 invitation/poster

02
Bunch Design
Eurotower 2
Invitation

1212
NYC

WWW.1212NYC.COM

AMSTERDAM AVENUE... THE AND... BIRD'S PLACE... BLACKOUT IN SIX...
BLACKOUT CROWD... AT RIVER MART... BLACKED OUT... CHINESE COUPLE...
FIRE ESCAPE... RAGU & 5TH... GIRL'S LOOK... DINERS VIEW... THE TOUCH
AT LAFAYETTE... SOME GRAFFITI... PARAMOUNT BUILDING... SOPHIANS &
DA CITY... MAGIC HOUR AT 42ND... LEAVIN' MANHATTAN... LOWER EAST...
SILHOUETTED SKYLINE... KIND ST. BLUR... BIKINI GIRLS... YELLOW CAB AT
HOTEL 41... COLORED... DUDE W/LADDER... EAST HOUSTON... HOMELESS
AT TIMES SQUARE... TINO... LITTLE ITALY... OLD ITALIAN... PROVE AT
PENTUTTI... GREEN AVENUE... GRAFFITI FACES...

US EMBASSY ZAGREB
GRADSKI URED ZA KULTURU
COCA-COLA
BUNCH
KATAPULT
DAPENAKEVA PIVOVARA
LABART
PROMO MEDIA

07.-15.10.2005

**MARIO DELIĆ I GALERIJA SC POZIVAJU
VAS NA OTVORENJE IZLOŽBE FOTOGRAFIJA
"1212NYC" U PETAK 07.10.2005. U 20,00 SATI
U GALERIJI STUDENTSKOG CENTRA
SAVSKA 25, ZAGREB.**

MARIO DELIĆ AND GALLERY SC INVITE YOU TO THE EXHIBITION "1212NYC"
ON FRIDAY 7TH, 2005 AT 8PM AT GALLERY SC, SAVSKA 25, ZAGREB

01

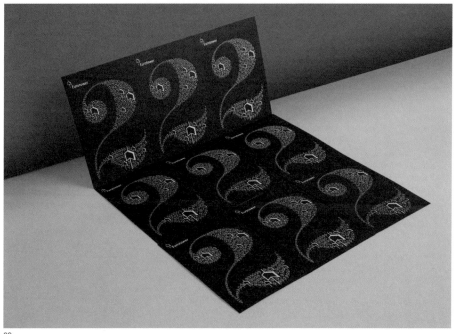

05.2.7
Vernacular:
Minimalism

A minimal photo shoot using four
fluorescent tube lights in the style of
the artist Dan Flavin was set up for the
album cover of *Pet Shop Boys – Disco
Four*, a collection of other people's
songs remixed by the Pet Shop Boys.
The inner sleeves feature different
permutations of the shoot as the lights
are progressively turned on and off.

01
Farrow Design
Photography by John Ross
Pet Shop Boys – Disco Four
Album cover and inner
sleeves

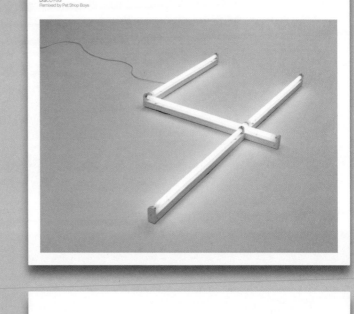

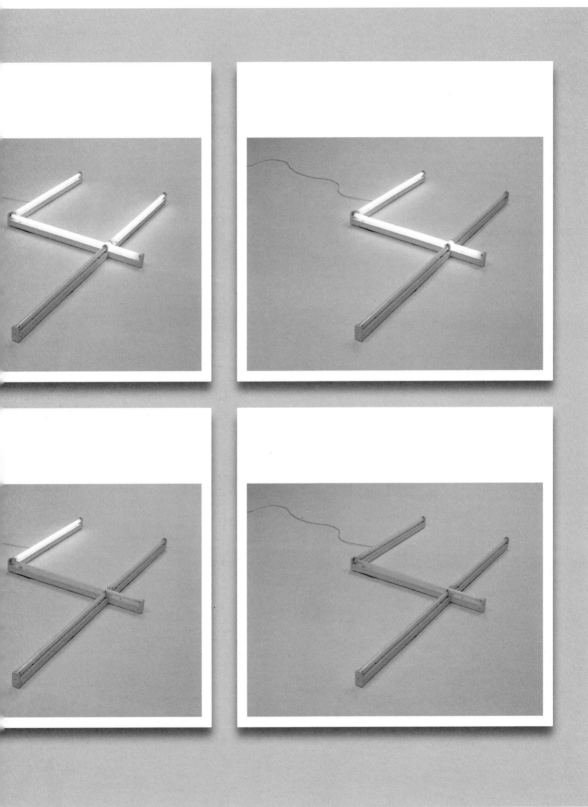

05.2.8
Vernacular:
Out of context

Form were asked to create covers for three singles and an album that would illustrate an underground feel, reflecting the tense yet light-hearted energy of the British garage band 187 Lockdown. The band did not wish to appear on the covers so a campaign was devised that revolved around a stark, graphic representation of its name. The designers focused on the 187 on a series of boards, and spent 12 hours with the photographer Spiros Politis shooting in locations around London that they felt represented the band's ethos. The boards were photographed in situ. This allowed for a distinctive identity over a series of covers.

The typography was industrial in feel and basic in its message: Neue Helvetica Bold caps, printed black on a process yellow background, emphasized the sense of tension with its 'hazard' Modernist delivery.

01
Form
187 Lockdown
Campaign for a British garage band: three singles and an album

187 LOCKDOWN.

A1: GUNMAN (ORIGINAL MIX)   00:06:19.
A2: SOUTHSIDE (ORIGINAL)   00:06:25.
A3: IT'S REAL (FEAT. SHOLA PHILLIPS)   00:06:02.
B1: YOUNG SON OF KUNG-FU   00:03:20.
B2: KUNG-FU (ORIGINAL 187 MIX)   00:06:26.
B3: THE WAH   00:06:11.
C1: NIGHTMARE ON 187TH STREET   00:06:18.
C2: IT'S IN YOUR EYES (FEAT. JANETTE SEWELL)   00:06:20.
C3: ALL 'N' ALL (FEAT. D'EMPRESS)   00:05:11.
D1: ROOM 1116   00:05:44.
D2: SOUTHSIDE (C-KEN REMIX)   00:05:56.
D3: THE DON   00:06:55.

05.2.8
Vernacular:
Out of context

87 formed part of Jonathan Ellery's first major solo show at the Wapping Project, London. Shown as a large installation piece with animation and sound, it looks at numbers out of context, enabling them to be seen in the abstract. An accompanying book was produced as a hand-numbered edition of 2000, 200 with a limited edition slip case. Each number in the sequence features a different typeface, including some strange and eclectic examples last spotted in Letraset catalogues from the 1970s.

02
Jonathan Ellery
87
Installation for the
Wapping Project

03
Jonathan Ellery
87
Exhibition catalogue

02

03

05.3.1
Type design:
Combined forms

Grandpeople's redesign for the Scandinavian fashion magazine *SVA* included the development of a new distinctive headline font Framtida, which was used for editorial titling and contents listings. Fragments of other fonts were pasted together to construct the characters. Several variations for most characters allow for greater variety on the printed page.

Pentagram created the identity and promotional material for 88 Morningside, a luxury residential building located on the Upper West Side of Manhattan. The concentric circular design of the 8s gives an almost abstract feel to the number.

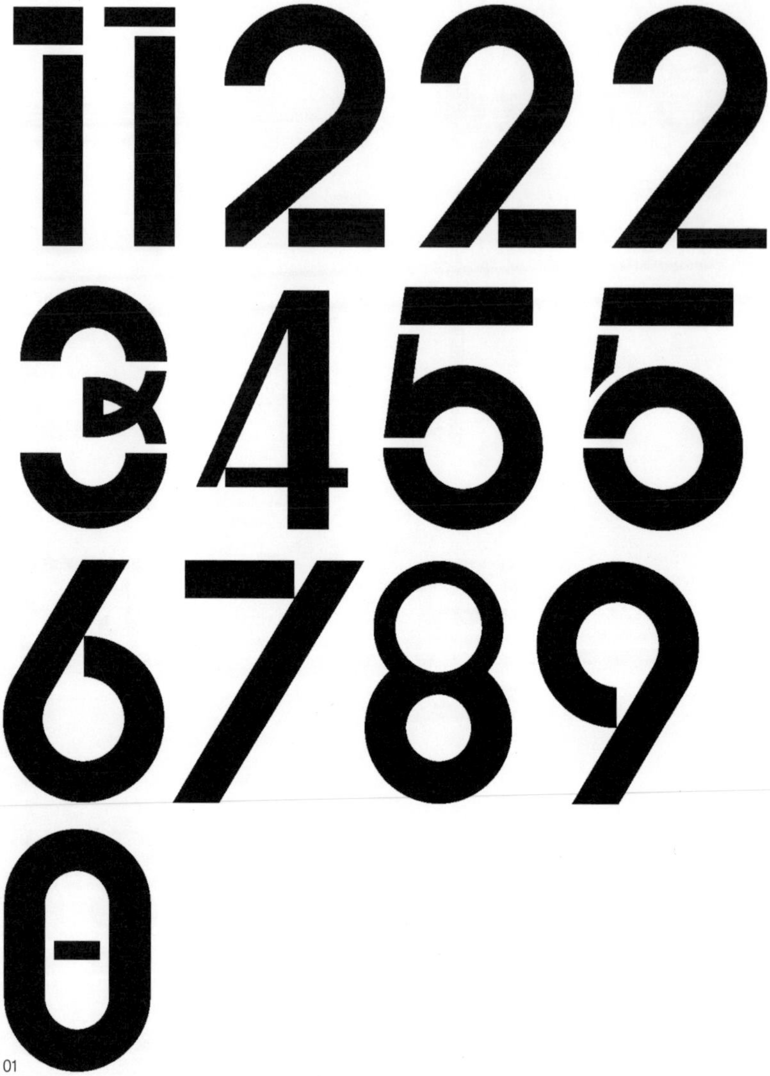

01
Grandpeople
Framtida Typeface
Type design for *SVA*
magazine

02
Pentagram
88 Morningside
Promotional brochure

01

05.3.2
Type design:
Abstraction

Stapelberg & Fritz have produced many experimental and challenging typfaces, with a strong focus on the numeric characters.

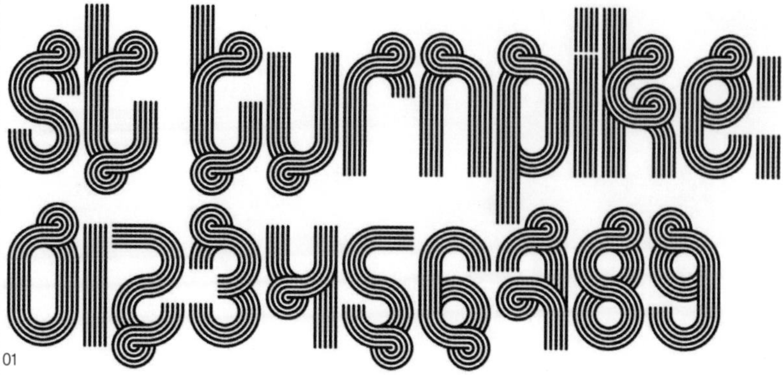

01

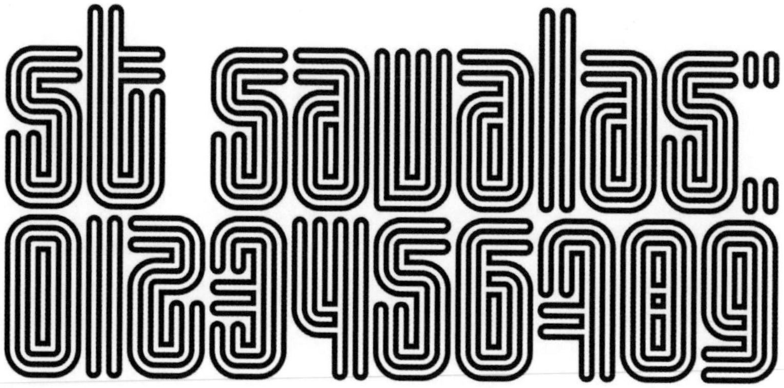

02

03

04

st bend.
0123456789

ot split::
0123456789

ot benner:
0123456789

05.3.3
Type design:
Numbers from letters

Eggers + Diaper worked on an exhibition project for the Jewish Museum Berlin called *10 + 5 = Gott* (*10 + 5 = God*)

The designers were intrigued by Hebrew because it has no numerals. Instead, the first letter of its alphabet, *aleph* is used for the numeral 1, the second letter *bet* is used for 2, etc. This means that Hebrew words can be seen simultaneously as a string of numbers.

In Hebrew 10 (*yod*) + 5 (*heh*) is 15, but it is also the word *yod-heh*, which is one of the many Hebrew words that represent 'God'. Hence the name of the exhibition. To reflect this duality in Hebrew, the designers developed a display face where the letters are made up of numbers or combinations of numbers.

01
Eggers + Diaper
10 + 5 = Gott
Type design and exhibition catalogue for the Jewish Museum Berlin

dans ville sembable, paru en 1972, Italo Calvino énumère, à la manière de fiches, les nombreuses villes ayant existé d'un bout à l'autre d'un empire (un empire ayant pris de telles dimensions que l'empereur lui-même n'en avait pas l'idée). Dans ce roman, les descriptions spécifiques des villes se suivent simplement, les unes après les autres. Sa forme est celle narrateur, Marco Polo, face à un auditeur, l'empereur, l'empereur qui se contente de l'exhorter à poursuivre son récit. Cette narration continue, donnée comme roman, transforme le lecteur en l'auditeur que fut l'empereur. Dans l'ensemble, aucune des histoires présentées au lecteur ne met en relation les villes entre elles et ne dit quoi ce soit de la structure générale de l'empire. Il est certain qu'à la lecture de ce livre, on ne pourra jamais dire « qu'un jour, un empereur a édifié un tel empire que… » ou que « chaque ville a sa propre forme et sa propre histoire ». À mesure que le lecteur s'enfonce dans le roman, la conscience lui vient du manque d'une ville qui s'est perdue dans sa mémoire ; ou bien, il s'égarera carrément dans la vastitude du texte. D'un côté comme de l'autre, sa conscience en tant que lecteur ne se fera pas à partir du contenu du roman, mais à travers l'acte même de lire.

SIGNS

PQRSTUVWXYZ

0 + 7   5   5   1   2   7   3   7+7   4   2

X JUMPS OVER THE LAZY DOG

7   1   2   3   6   5   0   7   5   1   4   3   1   6   2   4   9   0   5

06.
Form

06.1.1
Graphic:
Interlinked

Artiva Design created a large-format
folded journal and wallet for *Lettera22*,
a publication created to celebrate the
life of the designer Adriano Olivetti.
The intertwined 2s were inspired
by the black-ink ribbons used in the
original iconic Lettera22 typewriter.

01
Artiva Design
Lettera22
Folded journal, poster
and DVD

06.1.2
Graphic:
Upfront indexing

Sammlung Philip Metz, an art catalogue for the Philip Metz Collection, includes a French-folded dust jacket.

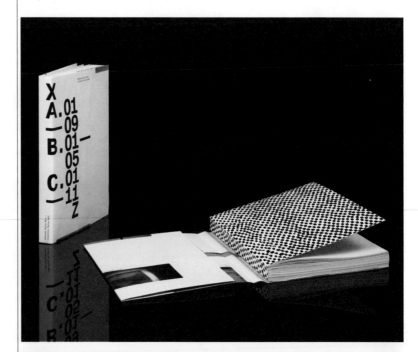

01
Stapelberg & Fritz
Sammlung Philip Metz
Art catalogue

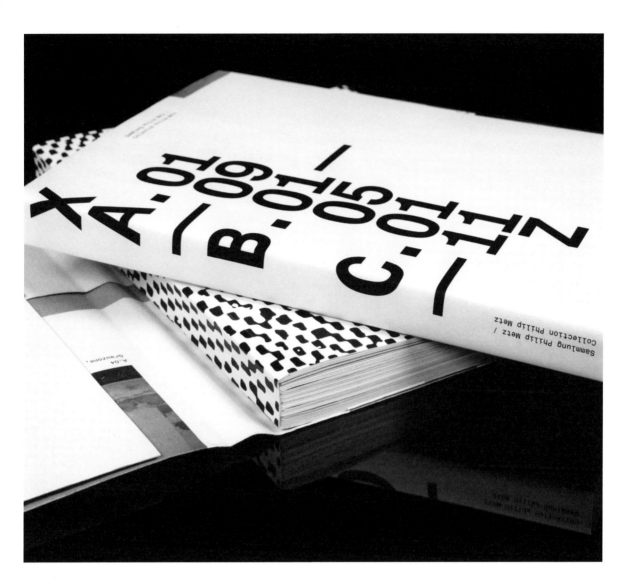

06.1.3
Graphic:
Type tests

SEA Design created a promotional
campaign celebrating the work
of seven great image-makers for
Naturalis, a range of papers from
Tullis Russell/GF Smith. Here, the
work of type designer Bruno Maag
is showcased.

Whereas previous editions were more
heavily image-based, this one focuses
on the designer's typeface Aktiv. The
x7 refers to the issue number, seven.

01
SEA Design
Naturalis
Tullis Russell/GF Smith
Promotional campaign, poster
and brochure design

Bruno Maag/Aktiv
Naturalis x7/GF Smith
Design SEA

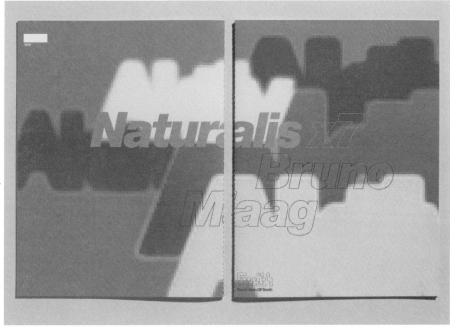

06.1.4
Graphic:
Number forms

Malcom Clarke's solution for a bespoke 30th anniversary invitation card for Grays antique centre in London was to affirm its position as a one-stop antiques emporium (with 200 individual sellers under its brand). This was achieved by using a pixel grid of 200 units at A5. Photographed objects from the multitude of sellers were placed in the grid to create a typographic/number image of 30.

Artiva Design created a large-format folded journal, poster and DVD wallet for *Dopo la rivoluzione*. The image here focuses on a typographic spread where the numbers are cropped in a way that reveals the negative spaces within the characters.

For the 20th Festival International de l'Affiche et du Graphisme de Chaumont in 2009, the organizing commitee invited 20 designers from around the world each to create a poster. Leonardo Sonnoli's design is a big number 20 composed of many elements from CMYK test strips. He created four versions of the poster, each printed in one colour: black, metallic bronze, fluorescent pink and reflex blue. Each version represents a different way to print.

01
Malcom Clarke
30th Anniversary of Grays Antiques
Invitation card

02
Artiva Design
Dopo la rivoluzione
Folded journal, poster and DVD

03
Leonardo Sonnoli
20th edition of the Festival International de l'Affiche et du Graphisme de Chaumont
Poster

01

02

**20e Festival International
de l'Affiche et du Graphisme
de Chaumont**
du 16 mai au 14 juin 2009

Ville de Chaumont.
Avec le soutien du Conseil général de la Haute-Marne,
du Conseil régional Champagne-Ardenne
et de la Direction Régionale des Affaires Culturelles /
Ministère de la Culture et de la Communication.

06.1.5
Graphic:
Interlaced

SEA Design created the identity
and poster for K2, one of London's
leading silk-screen print studios. The
characters K and 2 are formed from
horizonal strips which are interlaced in
various colourways and combinations
to create a flexible and varied identity.

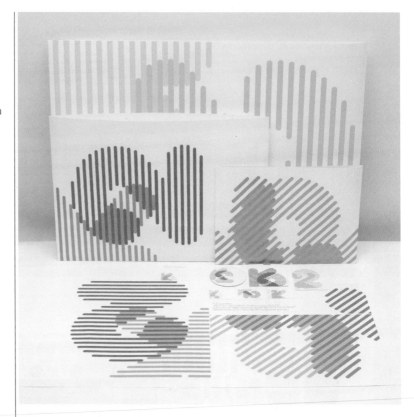

01
SEA Design
K2
Identity and poster

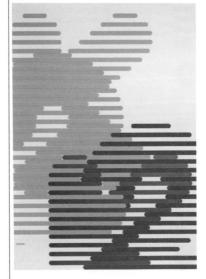

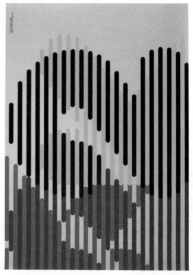

K2 Screen/Team
Edition 100/Design SEA

06.1.5
Graphic:
Interlaced

Remake Design's cover for the annual
report of Volunteer Lawyers for the
Arts illustrates the fact that the report
spans two years. The previous year's
number is graphically reduced through
the use of fine diagonal linework, with
the current year emboldened with
thicker lines. The two numbers are
then overlayed.

Thompson Brand Partners' 2009
and 2011 New Year cards for the
printers Kingsbury Press combine foil
blocking, embossing and conventional
lithography, and form a mini showcase
for the company's printing skills and
varied techniques. The letter forms are
interlaced with background linework.

01
Remake Design
*Volunteer Lawyers for
the Arts*
Annual report cover

02, 03
Thompson Brand Partners
Kingsbury Press 2009
New Year cards

04
Thompson Brand Partners
Kingsbury Press 2009
Diary

05, 06
Thompson Brand Partners
Kingsbury Press 2011
New Year cards

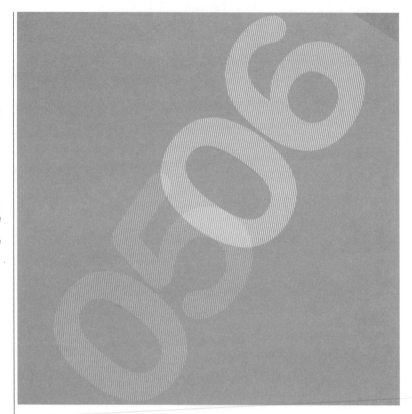

01

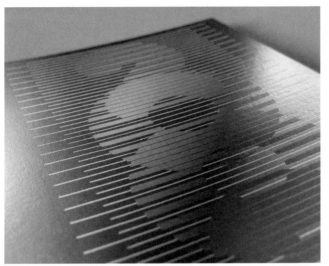

02

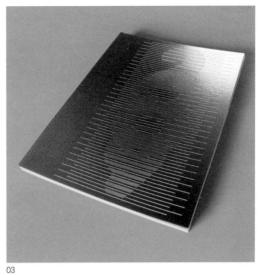

03

05

04

06

06.1.6
Graphic:
Cut and cropped

The Palau Foundation houses a significant documentary and bibliographical collection on Picasso, directed at national and international audiences. It also organizes temporary exhibitions. For the foundation's fifth annual art catalogue the Palau identity which employs a stylized stencil font, is extended into 03-08. The foundation was established in 2003; 2008 is when the catalogue was produced.

4257 is the title of the in-house magazine for the Japanese pharmaceuticals company Taiho. Helmut Schmid designed the identity and covers. The logo is formed from specially drawn interlocking numerals.

01
Marnich Associates
*Fundació Palau Fifth
anniversary art catalogue
and brochures*
The Palau Foundation

02
Helmut Schmid
4527
Taiho Pharmaceuticals
in-house magazine

01

03-08

Cinc anys de Fundació
2003-2008

palau 03-08

FUNDACIÓ PALAU
CENTRE D'ART
Caldes d'Estrac

...ersari
...ma d'activitats

palau 03-08

FUNDACIÓ PALAU
CENTRE D'ART
Caldes d'Estrac

06.1.7
Graphic:
Typographic limits

The ISIA (Istituto Superiore Industrie Artistiche) is the oldest graphic design university in Italy. It's located in the beautiful Renaissance village of Urbino in the central part of the country.

To promote its courses Leonardo Sonnoli designed a series of five number-based posters. Printed front and back, each one features a different typographic treatment for the numbers 3 and 2: the three years for a Bachelor degree and the two years for a Masters. Printed in black on five different coloured papers, the posters are designed to be hung so that 3 and 2 appear side by side.

01
Leonardo Sonnoli
ISIA Posters
Poster series

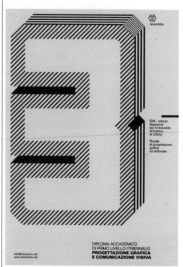

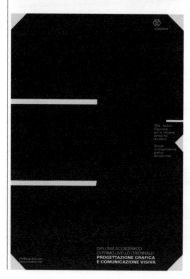

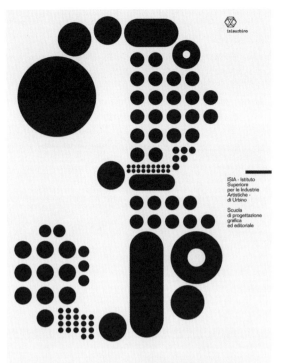

ISIA - Istituto
Superiore
per le Industrie
Artistiche -
di Urbino

Scuola
di progettazione
grafica
ed editoriale

DIPLOMA ACCADEMICO
DI PRIMO LIVELLO (TRIENNALE)
**PROGETTAZIONE GRAFICA
E COMUNICAZIONE VISIVA**

info@isiaurbino.net
www.isiaurbino.net

ISIA - Istituto
Superiore
per le Industrie
Artistiche -
di Urbino

Scuola
di progettazione
grafica
ed editoriale

DIPLOMA ACCADEMICO
DI SECONDO LIVELLO (BIENNALE)
→ **COMUNICAZIONE E DESIGN PER L'EDITORIA**
→ **FOTOGRAFIA DEI BENI CULTURALI**

info@isiaurbino.net
www.isiaurbino.net

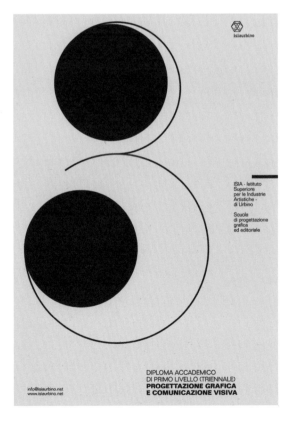

ISIA - Istituto
Superiore
per le Industrie
Artistiche -
di Urbino

Scuola
di progettazione
grafica
ed editoriale

DIPLOMA ACCADEMICO
DI PRIMO LIVELLO (TRIENNALE)
**PROGETTAZIONE GRAFICA
E COMUNICAZIONE VISIVA**

info@isiaurbino.net
www.isiaurbino.net

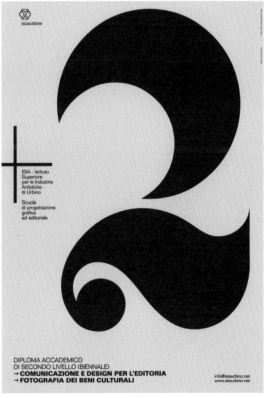

ISIA - Istituto
Superiore
per le Industrie
Artistiche -
di Urbino

Scuola
di progettazione
grafica
ed editoriale

DIPLOMA ACCADEMICO
DI SECONDO LIVELLO (BIENNALE)
→ **COMUNICAZIONE E DESIGN PER L'EDITORIA**
→ **FOTOGRAFIA DEI BENI CULTURALI**

info@isiaurbino.net
www.isiaurbino.net

06.1.8
Graphic:
Die-cut fragments

Struktur Design's *Units* consists of
two identical wire-bound wall-hung
calendars, each of which contains
ten sheets from 0 to 9. The user
turns these over to reveal the current
date. Each sheet is printed on a
different coloured card, and die cuts
are positioned in such a way that the
numbers reveal further fragments of
other numbers, and there is a small
trangular hole all the way through,
from the front sheet to the wall behind.

01
Struktur Design
Units
Die-cut calendar

06.2.1
Digits:
Forty-five degrees

Lend Lease, a leading retail
and residential property group,
commissioned Cartlidge Levene to
produce a series of three-dimensional
graphic interventions to inspire and
engage both staff and visitors. A
collection of framed environments was
created in different colours for each
floor of the company's new London
head office. Stencil-based numbers
were cut from the surface of these
boxes to create a sense of depth and
space. Other boxes in the clusters
can be filled with a variety of images
selected by members of staff.

Artiva Design's identity manual for the
Swedish energy company 45° reduces
the concept to its purest form – a line
set at a 45-degree angle.

01
Cartlidge Levene
Lend Lease
Floor numbering
intervensions

02
Artiva Design
45°
Identity manual

01

06.2.2
Digits:
Numeric history

The first settlers are believed to have arrived in Iceland in the ninth century: the oldest relics of human habitation found in Reykjavik and Krysuvik have been carbon-dated to about 871. The identity and catalogue here focus on this important date, and the graphics for *Reykjavic 871+/-2: The Settlement Exhibition* are treated in a fresh and contemporary manner as a contrast to the historial artefacts.

01
Atelier Atli Hilmarsson
*Reykjavik 871+/-2: The
Settlement Exhibition*
Identity, exhibition graphics
and catalogue design

Reykjavík Landnámssýningin
871 ±2 The Settlement Exhibition

Sýningin er opin alla daga frá 10–17

Minjasafn Reykjavíkur

The exhibition is open daily 10–17

Reykjavík City Museum

06.2.3
Digits:
Order and information

For the past decade, SEA Design have worked alongside GF Smith on its identity and literature systems for all product promotions in print and on the Web.

As the name suggests, *Master Selector* is a comprehensive literature system. It comprises an outer clam-shell box that houses two information books and a set of four small paper-sample books which show the company's entire range of papers. The large silver-foil-blocked numbers on the front of each of the sample books help to give a sense of order to the whole package.

01
SEA Design
Master Selector
GF Smith paper selector
information package

06.2.4
Digits:
Hero numbers

2009 marked the tenth anniversary of Fire Station Artists' Studios, a Dublin-based studio and workshop. Atelier David Smith employed a bold stencil numeric motif for the outer front cover of the book that was produced to mark the event.

Tara Mines is the largest lead and zinc mine in Europe and one of the biggest in the world. For over 30 years it has mined and extracted lead and zinc ore on the outskirts of Navan, County Meath. In 2008 and 2009 artist Tim Durham had unique access to all areas of the mine, and photographed both above ground and below in the light that was available. The resulting record of industrial landscapes and interiors formed an exhibition at the Solstice Arts Centre. The accompanying book, *650–1575*, takes its name from the depth of the mine. The large bold numbers that wrap around the book form a striking cover. The digits bleed off its foot to illustrate the notion of going underground.

Raw Alternatives, a poster that called for entries to a student design competition in 2003, focuses on a large 03.

01

01
Atelier David Smith
10th Anniversary Book
Fire Station Artists' Studios

02
Atelier David Smith
650–1575: Images of a Mine
By Tim Durham
Solstice Arts Centre

03
Atelier David Smith
Raw Alternatives
National Student Design
Competition poster

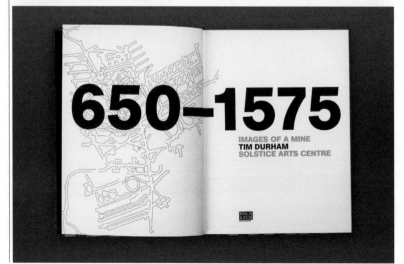

02

Designers Choice

RAW ALTERNATIVES NATIONAL STUDENT DESIGN COMPETITION

www.rawalternatives.com

www.terreus.com

03

The competition is open to all final year and penultimate year students on a registered graphic design or visual communications course in the Republic of Ireland and Northern Ireland.

The brief is available online or from Heads of Departments and Course Tutors. Students can register their interest at www.rawalternatives.com.

The competition is sponsored by Designers Choice, (the specialty division of McNaughton Paper, Ireland) and Terreus² the premium range of paper from Designers Choice.

The competition is supported by the Institute of Designers in Ireland (IDI) and Graphics International Magazine.

The overall winner will receive a cheque for €1000 from the sponsor. The winning student and two runners-up will be awarded certificates of excellence by the judging panel.

Winning entries will be showcased in Graphics International magazine and exhibited online at www.rawalternatives.com

The judges for this years competition are Conor Clarke (Design Factory), Lisa Godson (The Sunday Times) and Tara Clarke (ZINC). Further details available online.

The deadline for entries is Friday 28th March 2003.

[designerschoice] Terreus® Graphics International

Hörður Lárusson branded his 30th
birthday with a logo based on the
number and wordplay of his age and
his nickname, Hö. Guests invited to
his birthday party received a badge
and a small booklet with the official
invitation and directions on how to
get to the party since it took place in
the Icelandic countryside. A flag was
produced to mark the location.

Another report for Volunteer Lawyers
for the Arts, designed by Remake
Design (also see page 216), the two
years covered by the annual report
are shown with the previous year's
number fading out and translucent,
and the current year emboldening.

Remake Design's brochure for the
industrial design firm Teague uses
large custom-designed numbers to
highlight the section divides.

04

04
Hörður Lárusson
3Ö
Branding for the designer's
30th birthday party

05
Remake Design
*Volunteer Lawyers
for the Arts*
Annual report cover

06
Remake Design
Teague
Brochure for the industrial
design firm, Teague

In our opinion, the most successful cabin architecture is a harmonious relationship between the airline brand and the aircraft manufacturer's expressions. The latter being subordinate to the former. Like a great gallery or museum space, we consider the cabin envelope as a platform or blank canvas that fully realises and enables the airline brand's message and expression.

Horizon up

06.2.4
Digits:
Hero numbers

Bibliothèque presented *Happy Birthday Massimo* to design legend Massimo Vignelli at Design Indaba on the occasion of his 80th birthday. The poster reappropriates the iconic 365-day perpetual calendar (31 spiral-bound panels that rotate each day to give the date) using the number 80. The poster currently hangs on the wall at Vignelli Associates, New York.

In 2010 Bunch Design helped the real estate investors Consultant Group start the New Year with new collateral. A screen-printed planner in an edition of 200 was produced with an interesting composition of the year's digits.

Pentagram created an identity and packaging for the ceramicist and designer Emily Johnson. Her work follows in the steps of her forefathers who founded Johnson Brothers five generations ago, in 1882. She and her father paid homage to their heritage when they formed a new ceramics company: 1882 Ltd.

07

07
Bibilothèque
Happy Birthday Massimo
Poster for a design legend

08
Bunch Design
Consultant Group 2010
Limited edition screen-printed planner

09
Pentagram
1882
Identity and packaging

08

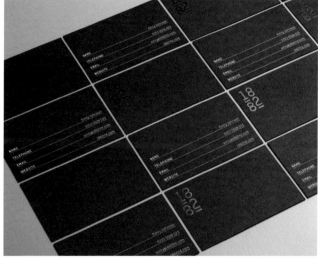

06.2.5
Digits:
Flamboyant typography

A spread from *Chic* magazine, designed by Marnich Associates, plays with the composition of the figures 3000cc. The strong elliptical space within the zeros creates a striking balance between the vertical and the horizontal.

A monograph for the French book designer and typographer Robert Massin features a numeric composition to indicate the six chapters in the book. Each chapter opener repeats the same composition, with the chapter number highlighted in white.

01
Marnich Associates
Chic magazine
Opening spreads from the fashion magazine

02
Struktur Design
Massin Chapter Openers
Monograph on the famous French graphic designer

01

La direction artistique

1 2 3 4 5 6

« Si vous me donnez carte blanche, je me chargerai de la typographie de tous les livres qui paraissent sous votre marque ». »

Le théâtre parlé

1 2 3 4 5 6

« [...] une pièce de théâtre risque de n'être qu'un corps sans vie si le typographe, entendant bien son rôle, ne s'emploie à donner à ce lecteur le sentiment que son fauteuil est celui d'un théâtre ». »

06.2.5
Digits:
Flamboyant typography

Leonardo Sonnoli's hand-drawn numerals for an advertisement for Petroltecnica uses seemingly abstract curvaceous elements to form the number 25.

The extreme contrast between thick and thin in the number 150 results in a beautiful piece of typography.

Issue 5 of *Elephant* magazine includes the four bespoke headline typefaces and one bespoke numeral set featured here.

03
Leonardo Sonnoli
25
Petroltecnica Terra Therapy

04
Leonardo Sonnoli
150
Hand-drawn typography

05
Studio8 Design
Elephant magazine
Title page and contents

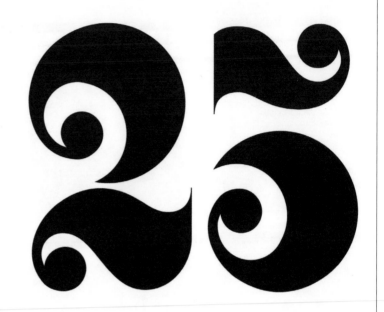

Petroltecnica / millenovecentottantacinque–
duemiladieci

03

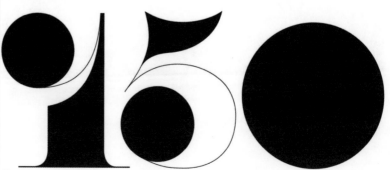

04

COLOPHON DISTRIBUTION

Editor-in-chief
Marc Valli
pvm@magmabooks.com

Editors
Ana Ibarra
ana@elephantmag.com

Margherita Dessanay
ma@elephantmag.com

Katya Tylevich

Fashion Editor
Julian Ganio
mfe@ludsungroup.com

Contributing Editors
Raphael Mathildo, Astrid Stavro

For all editorial enquiries:
Elephant Magazine
c/o Magma
117-119 Clerkenwell Road
London, EC1R 5BY

Design & Art Direction
Matt Willey (Studio8 Design)

Publisher
Swen Heuberts
peter@elephantmag.com

Sales & distribution
Benjamin Verhoefen
benjamin@elephantmag.com

Advertising
United Kingdom:
Sharon Joines
sharonjoines@gmail.com

Germany:
Pádraic Dolan
padim@elephantmag.com

All other areas:
Peter Heuberts
peter@elephantmag.com

Subscriptions
subscriptions@elephantmag.com
www.elephantmag.com

Subscription rates
EUR/CAN/USA
1-year €64.99
1-year student €54.99

How to subscribe?
Visit elephantmag.com
or call +31 20 4555 717

Elephant is published quarterly
by Frame Publishers BV
Laan der Hesperiden 68
1076 DX Amsterdam
The Netherlands
T +31 20 4233 717
F +31 20 4280853
www.elephantmag.com

All rights reserved.
Copyright © 2010 Frame
Publishers, Amsterdam, and
the individual contributors.
ISBN 2859 3635

Front cover
Valero Doval
from Aeroplane series
Digital Collage, 2010
(no pages 82-83)

Australia
Speedimpex Australia
T +61 2 9648 4922
F +61 2 9648 7775
info@speedimpex.com.au

Austria
Morawa Pressevertrieb
T +43 1 5156 2197
F +43 1 5156 2180 955
relationes@morawa.com

Belgium
IMAPress
T +32 14 40 38 98
F +32 14 42 50 67
info@imapress.be

Exhibitions International
T +32 16 296300
F +32 16 298200
info@exhibitionsinternational.be

Brazil
Freebook
T +55 11 3068 0577
F +55 11 3259 1140
informa@freebook.com.br

Canada
LMPI
T +1 514 355 5674
mmx14@msn.com

Cyprus
Naxis
T +357 96 145115
nfx@mainkiosk.com

Denmark
Interpress Danmark
T +45 3327 7764
F +45 3327 7701
cff@interpressdanmark.dk

Dubai
Tawedi Retail Distribution
T +971 4244 1016
info@tawedi.com

Finland
Akateeminen Kirjakauppa
T +358 9 121 5190
F +358 9 121 4416
post.sanomat@stockmann.fi

France
OFR Systeme International
T +33 1 4245 7288
F +33 1 4208 3478
ofrsystem@yahoo.com1

Germany
IPS Pressevertrieb
T +49 2225 8801 161
F +49 2225 8801 3280 81
info@ips-d.de

Vier Vier Vertrieb
T +49 3081 6094 98
info@vier-viertel-vertrieb.de

Greece
Papasotiriou Bookstores
T +30 10 9395 308
F +30 10 9848 364
diafontepaulia@papasotiriou.gr

Hong Kong
The Grand Commercial Co. Ltd.
T +852 2 3572639
F +852 2 570 9883
chagranda@i-cable.com

Hungary
IPS Pressevertrieb
T +49 2225 8801 161
F +49 2225 8801 3280 81
info@ips-d.de

India
RBD Subscription Services
T +91 11 2821 2258
F +91 11 2871 1008
rbd@vsnl.net.in

Indonesia
Basheer Graphic Books
T +65 6336 0321
info@basheergraphic.com

Italy
Idea Books SRL
T +39 0245 478 374
F +39 0245 477 784
imp@ideabooks.it

Japan
Motoses
T +81 6 6461 1618
F +81 6 6258 4880
info@motoses-co.jp

Malaysia
Basheer Graphic
T +65 6336 0321
info@basheergraphic.com

Middle East
AA Studio
T +961 1 990 293
F +961 1 990 293
aastudio@inco.com.lb

Netherlands
Betapress
T +31 161 457 800
F +31 161 453 161
m.matran@betapress.audax.nl

New Zealand
Map Nation
T +64 9 3669216
info@mapnation.com

Norway
Lotto AR
T +46 8 749 46 68
cerola.person@lotto.se

Portugal
International News Portugal
T +351 21 898 1010
marta.dias@internews.com.pt

Poland
IPS Pressevertrieb
T +49 2225 8801 161
F +49 2225 8801 3280 81
lutz/ing@IPS-Pressevertrieb.de

Serbia
Arbooks
T +381 11 24 57 083
F +381 63 23 42 906
office@arbooks.net

Singapore
Basheer Graphic Books
T +65 6336 0321
info@basheergraphic.com

South Africa
Magazine
T +27 11 579 1060
info@magazine.co.za

South Korea
TVM
T +82 2 391 8746
F +82 2 384 5341
exim@tqm.co.kr

Spain
Promotora de Prensa
International SA
T +34 227 931 484
F +34 932 634 883
evelissequent@promopress.es

Sweden
Svenska Interpress AB
T +46 8 5065 0651
suzette.pettersson@interpress.se

Switzerland
IPS Pressevertrieb
T +49 1225 8801 161
F +49 2225 8801 3280 81
lutz/ing@IPS-D.de

Thailand
Basheer Graphic Books
T +66 2391 9815
thai@basheergraphic.com

Taiwan
Long Sea
T +886 2 2706 6838
F +886 2 2706 6029
eric@longsea.com.tw

United Kingdom
COMAG
T +44 01895 433 173
F +44 01895 433 602
hazel.leuzon@comag.co.uk

United States
COMAG
T +44 01895 433 173
F +44 01895 433 602
hazel.leuzon@comag.co.uk

ELEPHANT
5
ISSUE   WINTER
2010 – 11

06.2.6
Digits:
Out of scale

Prill Vieceli Cremers' book *Stadion Letzigrund Zürich*, produced to commemorate the opening of the new sports stadium, uses page numbers that vary in size, from half a page down to more modest proportions, as a key aspect of the page design. The use of large numbers has a strong association with all types of sporting events, where they are seen pinned to the backs of athletes and on large scoreboards.

01
Prill Vieceli Cremers
Stadion Letzigrund Zürich
Book design

115

Stefan Frey, Res Mezger, Saro Pepe

Achtzig Jahre Letzigrund
Geschichten und Höhepunkte

Stefan Frey, Res Mezger and Saro Pepe

Eighty Years of the Letzigrund
Tales and Highlights

151

Am 22. November 1925 – in einer Zeit, als der Fussball zum beliebtesten Publikumssport avancierte – wurde die Heimstätte des FC Zürich erbaut. Am 21. August 2006 fand die offizielle Abbruchparty statt. Dazwischen liegen rund 80 Jahre Sportgeschichte, zu der nicht nur zahlreiche nationale und internationale Begegnungen des FC Zürich, sondern auch der erste Cupfinal in der Geschichte des Schweizer Fussballs sowie 24 Leichtathletik-Weltrekorde gehören.

1925 – das Stadion als Prestigebau
Am 22. November 1925 konnte der FC Zürich sein neues Heimstadion eröffnen: den Letzigrund. Das im Gebiet «An der Herdern», unmittelbar jenseits der damaligen Stadtgrenze in der Vorortgemeinde Altstetten gelegene Stadion bot auf einer kleinen Holztribüne und auf Stehrampen insgesamt 25'000 Zuschauern Platz. Die Presse geizte nicht mit Lob für das neue Stadion, das auch über eine 400-Meter-Aschenlaufbahn sowie eine Sprung- und eine Wurfanlage verfügte: Der Letzigrund sei eine «mustergültige Anlage», der «in der Schweiz wohl nur wenige von gleichem Ausmass und sportgemässer Konstruktion an die Seite gestellt werden können».[1] Gleichzeitig mit dem Letzigrund entstanden in der ganzen Schweiz neue Stadien. Zwischen 1922 und 1934

On 22 November 1925, at a time when football was becoming the most popular spectator sport, the home ground of the FC Zürich (FCZ) team was opened. The official demolition party took place on 21 August 2006. Between those dates lie roughly eighty years of sporting history, which covers not only numerous national and international matches for FC Zürich but also the first cup final in the history of Swiss football and twenty-four world records in track and field.

1925 – The Stadium as Status Symbol
FC Zürich opened its new home stadium, the Letzigrund, on 22 November 1925. The site, known as "An der Herdern", lay just beyond the municipal border at that time, in the suburb of Altstetten. The stadium had capacity for 25,000 visitors seated on a small wooden grandstand and standing on the terraces. The press did not stint with praise for the new stadium, which had a 400-metre cinder track as well as areas for jumping and throwing events. The Letzigrund was said to be an 'exemplary facility' to which 'surely few sports facilities of its size in Switzerland could be compared'.[1] New stadiums were being built throughout Switzerland at the same time. Twelve facilities with a capacity of over 10,000 were built between 1922 and 1924. Football experienced a leap in popu-

06.2.7
Digits:
Numbers as image

The Japanese mail-order company Askul offers more than 40,000 items with nationwide delivery within 24 hours. The service covers a variety of products ranging from furniture, stationery and computers to food and everyday commodities. Stockholm Design Lab redesigned 50 to 60 key products within this range. Their aim was to distinguish the products in a clear and graphical way: clarity equals more sales. The key was to find and use symbols that are easy for customers to understand at first glance. Examples are the sizes (1 to 4) for the batteries and the graphic numbers 6 and 7 that illustrate pads of lined notepaper available in 6mm and 7mm line spacing.

A series of booklet covers that Helmut Schmid produced for Hinex let the large-number sequence play the leading role: the number and all other typography are set at a 25-degree angle to create dynamic tension on the covers.

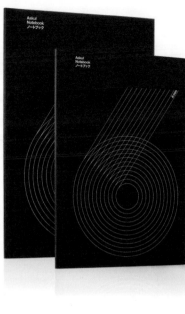

01

01
Stockholm Design Lab
Askul
Lined notebooks

02
Stockholm Design Lab
Askul
Battery design

03
Helmut Schmid
Hinex
Booklet covers

02

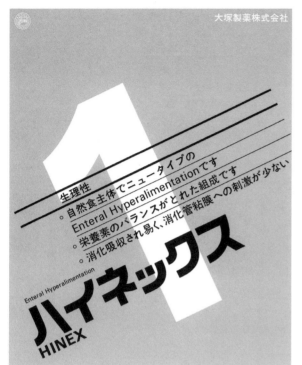

生理性
○ 自然食主体でニュータイプの Enteral Hyperalimentation です
○ 栄養素のバランスがとれた組成です
○ 消化吸収され易く、消化管粘膜への刺激が少ない

Enteral Hyperalimentation
ハイネックス
HINEX

有効性
○ 高カロリー補給が可能です
○ タンパクの利用がスムースです
○ 脂質代謝に好影響を与えます

Enteral Hyperalimentation
ハイネックス
HINEX

安性性
○ 長期投与が可能です
○ 長期保存が可能です
○ 副作用の頻度が従来製品と比較して非常に少ない

Enteral Hyperalimentation
ハイネックス
HINEX

便利性
○ 優れた流動性を有しています
○ 調製が容易です
○ 保存が容易です

Enteral Hyperalimentation
ハイネックス
HINEX

06.2.7
Digits:
Numbers as image

More examples of package design work for the Japanese mail order company Askul by Stockholm Design Lab demonstrate that while, above all, the designers' aim was to create a good, functional design, they also wanted to take away all unnecessary details and add an element of fun. The packaging of various office stationery items is reminiscent of pharmaceutical packaging from the 1960s and 1970s when a clear, restrained, international-design style was embraced.

The design of the USB memory sticks again reduces everything down to a great palette of colours and a large clear number stating the gigabytes of space contained on each stick.

04, 05
Stockholm Design Lab
Askul
Various stationery items

06, 07
Stockholm Design Lab
Askul
1, 2, 4 and 8GB USB sticks

04

06

05

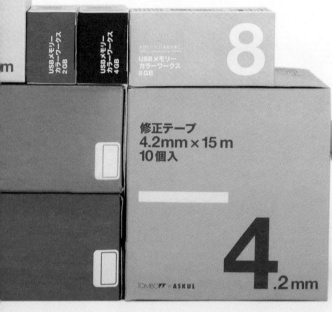

USBメモリー
カラーワークス
2GB

USBメモリー
カラーワークス
4GB

USBメモリー
カラーワークス
8GB

8

修正テープ
4.2mm×15m
10個入

4
.2mm

TOMBOW × ASKUL

Askul
オリジナルふせん
のりワイド
75×75mm

USBメモリー
カラーワークス
1GB

1

USBメモリー
カラーワークス
2GB

2

USBメモリー
カラーワークス
4GB

4

USBメモリー
カラーワークス
8GB

8

Graphic Design Essentials is a
simple step-by-step guide that helps
designers to familiarize themselves
with the basics in design software
programs. Large numerals are used to
depict the eight sections of the book.
The list of contents, which extends
over four pages, uses supersized
numbers for each chapter. The same
numbers are then repeated for the
cover design.

01
Struktur Design
Graphic Design Essentials
Book cover and contents

Graphic Design
Essentials:

Skills, Software, and Creative Solutions

Joyce Walsh Macario

1

Introduction

2

The Elements of Design

3

Typography

4

Images

5

Layout

6

Logo Design

7

Visual Themes

8

Information

A specially commissioned headline font was created by Commercial Type for an issue of *Bloomberg Businessweek* designed by Working Format. The font, which is constructed from concentric and parallel lines, is used at larger sizes and bleeds off the page. Even at these sizes the font maintains a light grey tonal value, and therefore does not overpower or conflict with the editorial content on the page.

01
Working Format /
Commercial Type
Bloomberg Businessweek
Custom type design

---

the challenges of a globalized world. Next, Germany and its neighbors imagined a unified Europe, and the country paid for it with spending power when the strong deutsche mark was retired for a then-weaker euro. Now Germans are paying again, to prevent Greece from pulling apart the European Union. It's a fresh reminder that togetherness has its costs–though 20 years later, the benefits of reunification speak for themselves.

Making What?
The *Heiss* List, page 70

What Drives the German Economy?
New Rules and Old Companies, page 72

Who's Earning, and Where?
The Workspace, page 76

Why Don't Germans Like Stocks?
Chronic Bubble Phobia, page 77

What Makes Saxony Run?
The Rebirth of Dresden, page 77

How Did Siemens Go From Scandal to Success?
"Never Miss a Good Crisis," page 79

How Does It Feel to Be a Turk in Germany?
A Merger in the Shadows, page 80

Plus: *Essential info on doing business in Germany –page 82*

6%

Percent of Germans who own stocks

1989 **200**

October 10, 2010
Businessweek

The Reichstag with Berlin Wall

The Reichstag, post-Wall

er, but it was also the start uring which Germans strug –nor just to each other but ble in Europe and their place rder. "It's like a marriage," Hohenthal, a former political nt for the German daily *Die* you start out, you are very , and even though you might d you aren't sure about ev– decide to do it. But eventu– ts in."

"r Unification"

e Berlin Wall did not make evitable. Although nominally , the two German states had xisted under the controlling e four victorious World War U.S., Great Britain, France, Union. As of 1989, hundreds of foreign troops, including million members of the Red

W. Bush. "We were the only ones besides the West Germans who were seriously in– terested in moving this thing."

The West Germans had doubts of their own. Helmut Kohl, the conservative Chan– cellor of the Federal Republic, told aides unification would take at least five years, if

opening, Kohl made a trip to Dresden, the bombed-out city that was still a part of the East. Throngs came out to cheer him and plead for German unity. "Kohl was not a great speaker, but he had a tremendous feeling for the people," says von Hohen– thal, who covered Kohl's trip for *Frank– furter Allgemeine Zeitung*, Germany's larg– est newspaper. "I remember looking at the faces of the people–they all were wear– ing black, red, and gold and chanting, 'Helmut, Helmut!' You could just sense that the East Germans were absolutely longing–screaming–for unification."

By the start of 1990 the Kohl govern– ment seized the opportunity and pushed for a rapid, one-state solution. The Sovi– ets presented the biggest dilemma: Let– ting go of the GDR, Moscow's most im– portant satellite in Central Europe, would be tantamount to conceding defeat in the Cold War. To exact agreement from the Soviets, Kohl turned to Bush, who per–

tails of how to unite the two states formal– ly and remove foreign troops were worked out through the "2+4" negotiations—in– volving representatives of the two Germa– nys, plus those from the four occupying powers—a process devised by Washing– ton to limit the circle of actors with a say over Germany's future. The final treaty reestablishing German sovereignty was drafted by the end of the summer and signed on Sept. 12, 1990, as– tonishingly quick by the glacial standards of international diplomacy.

The negotiators had glossed over the consequences for the citizens of the GDR, many of whom were unprepared for the coming transformation of their way of life. Yet it's difficult to see how it could have happened any other way. Within a year of the Moscow treaty, Gorbachev was pushed out of power by hardliners in the Kremlin. The Soviet empire collapsed. Ne– gotiating with more mercurial figures in

living conditions in much East Germany show few sig ment. With the disappear nal borders, some 2 mill mans moved west, sapping what little intellectual capi cal knowhow it had left.

519

Number of Olympic medals East Germany won, from 19 to 1988. West Germany won 253.

October 4 — October 10
Bloomberg Busines

When soccer player Mesut Ozil scored for Germany at the 2010 World Cup in South Africa, fans back home didn't care where his parents were from. Cem Ozdemir, whose Turkish-born mother once worked as a seamstress in south– ern Germany, became the nation's first federal lawmaker from an immigrant family in 1994 and now heads the op– position Green Party, which is polling at a record high.

Turkish-Germans run some 80,000 businesses that employ, on average, five people. Still, they're only about half as likely as Germans to start companies, according to the Turkish Community in Germany, an advocacy group.

Driving anti-immigrant sentiment is a large, unassimilated Turkish underclass.

community has the lowest share of high school graduates (14 percent) and an un– employment rate of 23 percent, accord– ing to a 2009 study by the Berlin Institute for Population and Development. That compares with a 7.6 percent jobless rate for Germany in August. Turks and their children are twice as likely as Germans to wind up on welfare, and in Berlin they top the police tally of gang criminals.

"Yes, there is discrimination" against non-German job seekers, says Nihat Sorgec, head of a vocational school in Berlin's heavily immigrant Kreuzberg neighborhood. "But whining and feel– ing victimized is not the best way to fight this. You need to move on and say, 'These are my qualifications, I can do this job better than others.'" His wish is

"We can't waste any talent." Asked non-Germans need to do to get al politicians from Merkel on down i Learn German. "Whoever lives amo also has to be ready to integrate in ciety, learn the language, particip school," Merkel said in August. "T a lot to do in that respect."

Turkish community leaders say mans need to be more welcoming. a decade ago politicians were still ing whether Germany was an "imr tion country" at all. In 2000, afte Social Democratic government of hard Schröder changed the country zenship law to reflect growing dive a leader of Merkel's Christian Demo called for a "guiding culture" of Ger ness. Another complicating factor

**Average salary of a worker
in the former East Germany,
vs. peers in the West:**

cating Merkel to rescue the system not because she loves Europe, but because Germany is its leading beneficiary.

While Kohl battled to keep German and European interests in perfect alignment, he was also the consummate domestic political opportunist. He dodged and weaved for months in 1990 before recognizing Poland's border with Germany as inviolable–the same kind of fence-straddling Merkel was accused of when Greece pleaded for help. And by the end of his tenure in 1998, Kohl, with his treasury buckling under the cost of subsidizing the East, was making idle threats to stop paying into the EU budget.

So when critics–including many

as the EU grew from 6 countries in 1957 to 15 in 1995, and it worked for the creation of the euro in 1999. But things are different in today's larger bloc. Defeats for German-French projects used to be rare; now they are increasingly common, as when other governments rejected France and Germany's argument for a European financial transaction tax on Sept. 7. "For a long time the German-French relationship has been much more appearance than reality," says Günter Verheugen, 66, Germany's EU commissioner from 1999 to 2010. "The days are gone when a German-French directorate could set the course of European integration."

It's not only a numbers game. German

abroad. Some 64 percent of that investment is in the EU, sustaining 2.9 million jobs, according to Deutsche Bundesbank data. "The export model directly benefits other countries," says Heleen Mees, a researcher at the Erasmus School of Economics in Rotterdam. "It's very worthwhile for those countries to have German factories and technologies."

Merkel has won on one point. As the EU tries to strengthen the euro region's financial management, the onus is on weaker countries to improve how they do things, not on Germany to abandon fiscal rigor and loosen the lid on wages. Yet that's about the only point she has taken so far. German calls for harsher

**Known number of people
between 1961 and 1989
who died attempting to
cross the Berlin Wall:**

omy Minister Sven Morlok. Two key figures in the transformation were Kurt Biedenkopf, now 80, the Christian Democrat who served as premier from 1990 to 2002, and the late Kajo Schommer, who served as economy minister during the same formative period. Together they developed a "lighthouse principle" in which industries with high potential–especially autos and microelectronics–got most of the state aid.

"The state's political and business leaders boosted the self-confidence of the Saxon people and convinced them their fate was in their own hands," says Joachim Ragnitz, managing director of the Ifo Institute for Economic Research

and his team," says Jens Drews, Globalfoundries' director of government relations. "They were visionaries."

With 4.2 million people, Saxony sits in an eastern nook of Germany, with the Czech Republic to the south and Poland to the east. Twenty years after reunification, about 6,000 companies have invested €27 billion ($35 billion) in the state, which is smaller than New Jersey. East Germany's anticommunist mass protests had their genesis in the Saxon city of Leipzig in 1989, paving the way for demonstrations that swept the hard-line state before it imploded that year. As a result, Saxon voters have not elected any former East German communist to power as part

cleaner and more prosperous, the church towers bigger and higher."

Porsche's plant is a symbol of the new Saxony, employing 640 people on the site of a former Soviet military training base. It churns out 250 Cayennes and 100 Panameras a day. The meticulous attention to detail that makes Saxons good at building Porsches is also an asset for producing luxury products such as watches and fine wine. A. Lange & Söhne, the watchmaker established in 1845 in the village of Glashütte near the Czech border, was expropriated by the communists in 1945 and reestablished in December 1990 by Walter Lange, a direct descendant of the founder. Jerzy Schaper, Lange's CEO, says watch-

06.3.2
Expression:
Focal points

Eggers + Diaper have designed the anniversary dinner invitations for the Jewish Museum Berlin for the past ten years. Each year the challenge is how to combine the anniversary number with the title. In most years the numeral replaces or is incorporated into a letter in the title. The colour palette of grey and red remains constant while the typographic treatments vary from year to year.

For the poster for the second Chicago International Poster Biennial, Pentagram used the number 2 as the main focus of the design. The spiralling white lines are based on rolled-up posters viewed from one end.

01
Eggers + Diaper
Anniversary Dinner
Invitations
The Jewish Museum Berlin

02
Pentagram
Second Chicago International
Poster Biennial 2010
Official poster

01

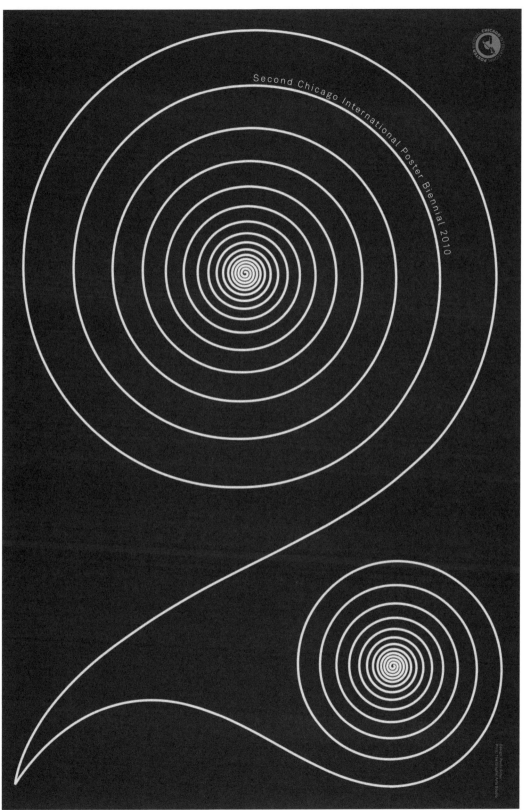

Second Chicago International Poster Biennial 2010

06.3.3
Expression:
Calligraphic

The identity for *3 at Saks Fifth Avenue*, on the third floor of the famous department store, was developed by Pentagram. The invitation card and identity beautifully intertwine all the key designer brand names to form an elegant number 3.

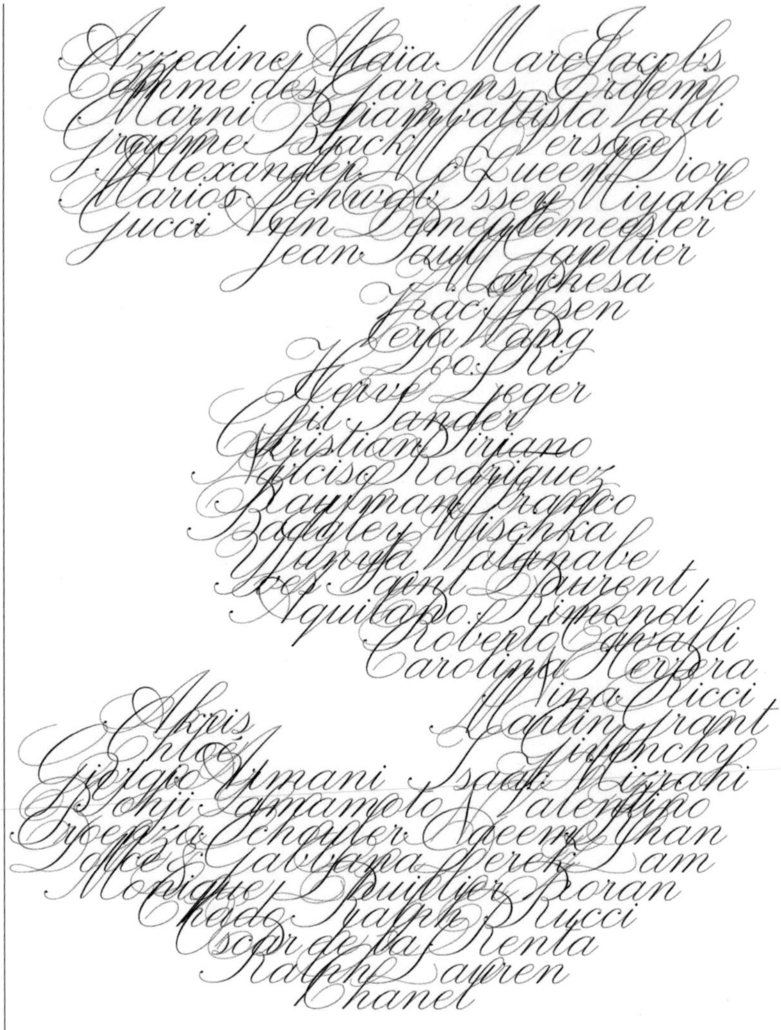

01
Pentagram
3 at Saks Fifth Avenue
Invitation for a new designer collection

06.3.4
Expression:
Forms from numbers

A 24th birthday card from gggrafik playfully turns the numerals into a swan gliding through the water.

For the tenth anniversary of the Italian edition of the men's magazine *GQ*, the editor asked ten international designers to supply covers. This is Leonardo Sonnoli's cheeky solution.

To announce a fifth anniversary party at the Russian Disco in Heidelberg, gggrafik created a poster with a reworked hammer and sickle, which are transformed into a number 5.

Nina feiert   Fr. 06.07.07   Ab 19:00 Uhr – Grill and Chill
24. Geburtstag   Im Weststadtcafé Darmstadt Fleisch selbst mitbringen, für alles andere ist gesorgt

01

01
gggrafik
24
Birthday card

02
Leonardo Sonnoli
GQ Italia
Cover design

03
gggrafik
Fifth anniversary
Russian Disco
Poster

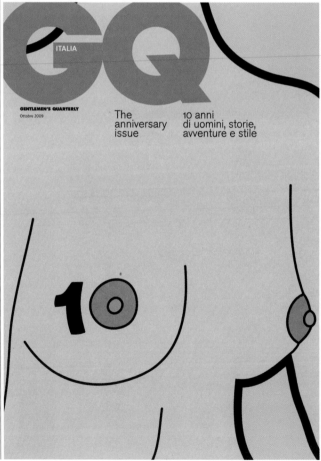

02

WLADIMIR KAMINER

FUENF JAHRE RUSSENDISKO

ZEHN JAHRE KARLSTORBAHNHOF

MI. 7.12. KARLSTORBAHNHOF
20.00 UHR LESUNG/22.00 UHR RUSSENDISKO

Grafix: Götz Gramlich, Druck: Glogner-Druck Heidelberg

06.3.5
Expression:
Colour play

Ich & Kar have developed the
identity system for the École de
Communication Visuelle (ECV)
in Lille, France, for a number of
years. Featured here are several
interpretations of years, displayed in
playful typographic combinations.
The palette and typography remain
the same but the interaction between
the digits evolves from year to year.

01

02

01
Ich & Kar
ECV
Identity, 2008

02
Ich & Kar
ECV
Identity, 2011

03
Ich & Kar
ECV
Identity, 2009

07.
Multiplication

**07.1.1
Signage systems:
*Number spaces***

The Alie Street signage is a building
identity and sign system that
makes use of prominent numbering
throughout for floor identification.
The clear large numbers are highly
visible throughout the building and are
counterbalanced by the more discreet
secondary information.

01
Commercial Art
Alie Street Signage
City of London Corporation
building

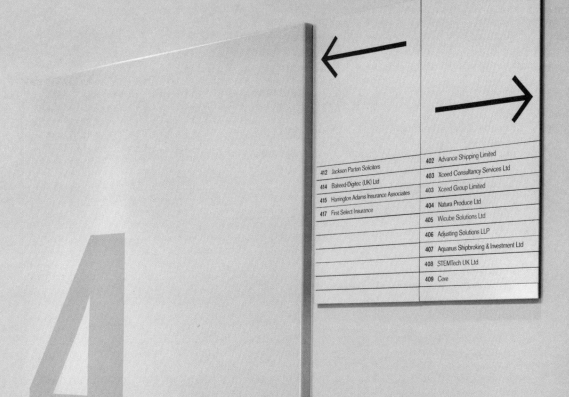

412	Jackson Parton Solicitors	402	Advance Shipping Limited
414	Bakeed-Digitec (UK) Ltd	403	Xceed Consultancy Services Ltd
415	Harrington Adams Insurance Associates	403	Xceed Group Limited
417	First Select Insurance	404	Natura Produce Ltd
		405	Wicube Solutions Ltd
		406	Adjusting Solutions LLP
		407	Aquarius Shipbroking & Investment Ltd
		408	STEMTech UK Ltd
		409	Core

4

07.1.2
Signage systems:
Architectural numbers

Pentagram created signage, environmental graphics and media installations for the corporate headquarters of Bloomberg, the financial news, data and analytics provider. The company occupies nine floors of a 55-storey tower on Manhattan's East Side.

Wayfinding in the building is coordinated by number. Each level is marked with an illuminated translucent colour-coded resin number encased in glass. The supersized floor numbering system extends to the emergency stairways, where oversized numbers are painted over walls and stairs.

01
Pentagram
Bloomberg
Wayfinding system

07.1.3
Signage systems:
Data streaming

The sixth floor of Bloomberg's
Manhattan headquarters includes an
area known as the 'Link', a three-
storey glass bridge that includes
the main entrance to offices and
communal terminals for staff and
guests. Here, the designers created
oversized news zippers that scroll on
three sides of the space, including a
media wall broken into four parallel
bands that capture data from the
Bloomberg live feeds. The flow
of information complements the
movement of people in the space,
and the changing colours of the
media wall transform the space
throughout the day.

01
Pentagram
Bloomberg
Live data-streaming

07.1.4
Signage systems:
Monochromatic

Large-scale outlined floor numbers
dominate the rough whitewashed
brick walls of an industrial building in
Metropolitan Wharf, Wapping, London.

01
SEA Design
Metropolitan Wharf,
Wapping, London
Signage system

07.1.5
Signage systems:
Life-sized

The identity work produced by April for the architectural practice John McAslan + Partners was extended to the company's new head office. The signage consists of a combined floorplan for all levels next to the reception area and the relevant number is repeated as a supergraphic on each floor. The huge numerals bleed into a solid panel of colour which includes information about the location of meeting rooms and other facilities.

01
April
John McAslan + Partners
Large-scale level indicators

THIRD FLOOR

STUDIO 3
MEETING ROOM 3

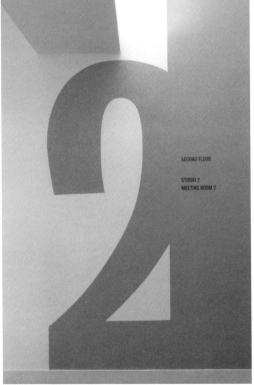

SECOND FLOOR

STUDIO 2
MEETING ROOM 2

07.1.6
Signage systems:
Numeric navigation

The signage and navigational system
for the Pass scientific adventures park
in Belgium works directly with raw
materials. Large panels are painted
bright colours that relate to on-screen
virtual navigation maps of the park.
Large-scale typography applied
directly to surfaces indicates zones
or levels. Set in the utilitarian font
DIN, the numbering system looks like
something from a space station.

01
Base Design
*Pass scientific
adventures park*
Signage and wayfinding
system

07.1.7
Signage systems:
Dot matrix

At Magnusson Fine Wine facility in Stockholm all wines are stored under optimal conditions in a modern environment. In addition to the storage services the facility offers a wine bar and a *chambre séparée* exclusively for members. Stockholm Design Lab has together with Thomas Eriksson Architects created a visual identity program and interiors for the facility in Stockholm. A clean minimal dot matrix font is employed throughout the storage facility, stencilled and printed to a variety of surfaces in a consistent manner.

The dot matrix also features in the signage at Bella Sky, Scandinavia's largest hotel. The hotel has created a distinct new profile on the Copenhagen skyline with the architecture of 3XN. The two leaning towers reach up to 76.5 metres. Stockholm Design Lab created the hotel's new identity and signage system. A unique typeface has been made, taking its inspiration from the architecture.

01

01
Stockholm Design Lab
Thomas Eriksson Architects
Magnusson Fine Wine
Signage and indexing system

02
Stockholm Design Lab
Thomas Eriksson Architects
Bella Sky
Hotel identity and signage system

02

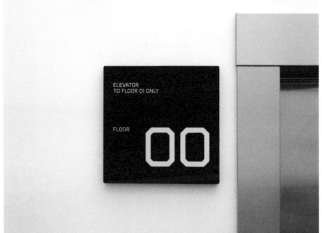

ELEVATOR
TO FLOOR 01 ONLY

FLOOR

00

1234567890

FLOOR

22

07.1.8
Signage systems:
Stencil shadows

Using a bold stencil font, Studio
Myerscough created a striking and
original solution for the wayfinding
system within the London College of
Communications. All the numbers are
black as this creates the strongest
contrast to the potential visual noise of
the busy corridors. The supergraphics
are made even more striking by
seeming to cast their shadows
across the floors, creating a three-
dimensional effect. The floor graphics
improve navigation of the site because
they are visible to anyone decending
the stairs.

01
Studio Myerscough
*London College of
Communications*
Wayfinding system

07.1.9
Signage systems:
Perspective

A 140m-long access corridor
connects the sections of the
new Kreissparkasse building in
Ludwigsburg. The perspective of the
floor level and staircase signs is so
distorted that they can only be viewed
from one point; otherwise they morph
into a game of free forms.

01
L2M3 Kommunikationsdesign
Kreissparkasse, Ludwigsburg
Three-dimensional morphing
signage system.

07.2.1
Supergraphics:
Supersized

Located in the heart of London, the Barbican Arts Centre has always been challenging to navigate. This signage and navigation system works in perfect harmony with the original 1960s concrete architecture. It utilizes a strong orange colour throughout, combined with Futura Bold set in lower case.

A key feature of the system is the use of superscale numerals positioned by the side of the lifts. These floor-to-ceiling numbers are cut out from the orange facia to reveal the original rough concrete walls.

In addition to the signage system, Cartlidge Levene produced a simple concertina-folded map to help visitors navigate the centre. The map uses the same large-scale numbers, printed as mirror images on the reverse of the thin paper.

01
Studio Myerscough/
Cartlidge Levene
Barbican Arts Centre, London
Wayfinding system

02
Cartlidge Levene
Map
Floorplan map

01

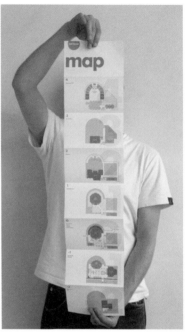

07.2.2
Supergraphics:
Beyond borders

This promotional information sheet
was produced to announce the fourth
Urban Prototyping Conference held
in the Institute of Architecture at the
University of Applied Arts in Vienna.
The A5 leaflet folds out into an A2
poster with a dominant number 4
filling the entire sheet.

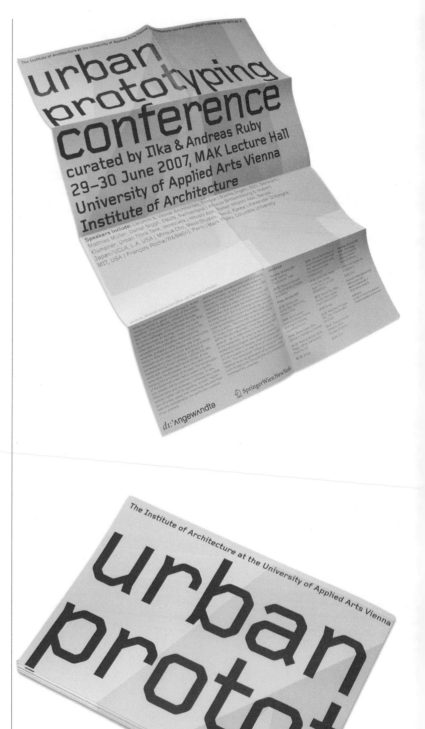

01
Paulus M. Dreibholz
*Urban Prototyping
Conference*
A2 folded information sheet

The Institute of Architecture at the University of Applied Arts Vienna and Architecture Live 4 present STADT = FORM RAUM NETZ Vol. 2:

urban prototyping conference

curated by Ilka & Andreas Ruby
29–30 June 2007, MAK Lecture Hall
University of Applied Arts Vienna
Institute of Architecture

Speakers include: Lacaton & Vassal Architectes, France | Bjarke Ingels, BIG, Denmark | Mathias Müller, Daniel Niggli, EM2N, Switzerland | Alfredo Brillembourg & Hubert Klumpner, Urban Think Tank, Venezuela | Hitoshi Abe, Atelier Hitoshi Abe, Sendai, Japan/UCLA, L.A. USA | Minsuk Cho, Mass Studies, Seoul, Korea | Alexander D'Hooghe, MIT, USA | François Roche/R&Sie(n), Paris | Mark Wigley, Columbia University

www.dieangewandte.at/archurban

While massive urbanization is on its way to "establishing a definitive, global 'triumph' of the urban condition" (Rem Koolhaas), urbanism as a profession has not evolved much in the past decades to fit the challenges of the contemporary city. What could have been an exciting venture into a new urban era in China has been mostly buried in the conventionalism of bloodless masterplanning schemes. Instead of using the current construction frenzy in Asia to test and develop new urban concepts which respond to the specifics of diverse contemporary urban conditions, a handful of masterplanning firms ruthlessly colonize the new world with outdated typological clichés. At the same time, the European city is more and more turning into a museum of its past. The conservation of the historical urban fabric seems to be the only mission left to urbanism in Europe. If new interventions are necessary, contemporary urban policies rather call for applying 'proven' typologies of urban space than inventing new ones that take into consideration the particular condition of our present.

Architects follow this development with a growing sense of alienation, as they are hardly asked to take part in the shaping of the contemporary cities. Apparently society does not hold architecture capable of making a useful contribution to our built environment that exceeds the limited realm of a building as such. But if according to Vitruvius a city is a big house and a house is a small city, any act of building inevitably contributes to the building of the city as a whole. The time has come for architects to reclaim their capacity and responsibility to define the city inductively – from the specific to the general – as an alternative to the deductive logic of the masterplan. In order to rejuvenate the established typological vocabulary of urbanism, architects need to develop urban prototypes which act as incubators of new forms of urban organization. The symposium "Urban prototyping" brings together a young generation of architects whose work foregrounds the potential of architecture for contemporary urbanism.

PROGRAM

Thursday, 28 June 2007
19:00 Opening
"The Essence", MAK

20:30 Party Architecture
Live 4, University of Applied
Arts Vienna

Friday, 29 June 2007

13:30 Introduction:
Gerald Bast, Wolf D. Prix,
Andreas Ruby

14:00 Anne Lacaton,
Lacaton & Vassal, France:
Grafting the Existing,
Upgrading the City

14:45 Bjarke Ingels, BIG,
Denmark: Developing Urbanism

15:30 Mathias Müller, Daniel
Niggli, EM2N, Switzerland:
Pimp my city

16:15 Break

16:45 Alfredo Brillembourg &
Hubert Klumpner, Urban Think
Tank, Venezuela: Metro Cable.
Architecture as Urban
Infrastructure

17:30 Hitoshi Abe, Atelier
Hitoshi Abe, Sendai,
Japan/UCLA, L.A. USA:
MEGAHOUSE

18:15 Minsuk Cho, Mass
Studies, Seoul, Korea:
Seoul Commune 2026

19:00 Break

19:30 Alexander D'Hooghe,
MIT, USA: Suburbia after
the Crash

20:15 François Roche/
R&Sie(n), Paris:
Entropic Urbanism

21:00 End

Saturday, 30 June 2007
10:00 Mark Wigley,
Columbia University:
Beyond Urbanism
(Keynote Lecture)

11:00 Final Debate with
all Speakers

13:00 End

The event takes place at the
MAK Lecture Hall
Weiskirchnerstraße 3
1010 Vienna, Austria

Admission:
€ 9.00 / € 4.00 (concession)
Tickets available at the event.

di:'ʌngewʌndtə   SpringerWienNewYork

07.2.2
Supergraphics:
Beyond borders

There is a clear sense of scale on the opening pages of the *Focus Open 2011* international design awards book (also see page 164). The typography, which was shot in a large studio setting, is seen to be constructed by an individual as he walks around adding panels of lettering to the titles.

SEA Design produced a large screen-printed poster to announce an exhibition and lecture showcasing their design work, held at Belfast University. The sense of scale is exaggerated by the highly cropped title and contrasting small typography.

02
Stapelberg & Fritz
Focus Open 2011
Book design

03
SEA Design
Belfast University
Exhibition/lecture poster

02

A
Talk
by
SEA /
Bryan
Edmondson

The
Lecture
Theatre

School
of
Art
+
Design

University
of
Ulster
Belfast

6.45pm

07.2.2
Supergraphics:
Beyond borders

Studio 468 is the address of an artist's
residency programme in Dublin. The
flysheet/dust jacket of a report on
the residency is folded to follow the
relative proportions of each panel
(4 units/6 units/8 units). The cropped
and sliced fragments of the numbers
create a strikingly dramatic typographic
solution for the cover.

04
Atelier David Smith
Studio 468
Folded report

07.2.3
Supergraphics:
Full frame

The Big Ten Conference is the oldest and largest Division I college athletic association in the United States. Pentagram designed a new logo featuring contemporary collegiate lettering with an embedded numeral 10 in the word BIG, which allows fans to see BIG and 10 in a single word.

70mm – Bigger than Life was a retrospective exhibition, held at the Museum of Film and Television in Berlin, of films shot on extra-wide 70mm film material. Pentagram accentuated the large scale of this format by printing an oversized number 70 which bleeds off the edge of the poster.

01
Pentagram
B1G
Re-branding for Big Ten

02
Pentagram
70 mm – Bigger than Life
Poster

01

RETROSPEKTIVE
5. BIS 15. 2. 2009

International, Karl-Marx-Allee
Cinestar 8, Potsdamer Straße

Vorträge und Gespräche
www.deutsche-kinemathek.de

59.
Internationale
Filmfestspiele
Berlin

DEUTSCHE
KINEMATHEK
MUSEUM
FÜR FILM UND
FERNSEHEN

70 mm – Bigger than Life

Gefördert durch

07.2.4
Supergraphics:
Three-dimensional digits

The signage and wayfinding system developed by Studio Myerscough for the Tea Building, a creative studio complex in Shoreditch, East London, is based on the stencilled serif lettering often found on tranditional tea crates.

Studio Myerscough also created *2020*, a handmade typographic sculpture, for a cover of the design magazine *ICON*. The white on white lettering, created as an anolgue version of bitmapped typography, relies on light and shade for legibility. *Number 2* explores this theme of three-dimensional bitmapped typography further, arranging different blocks of coloured wood to form the number 2.

01

01, 02
Studio Myerscough
Tea Building
Signage and wayfinding
system

03
Studio Myerscough
2020
Cover for *ICON* magazine

04
Studio Myerscough
Number 2
Prototype three-dimensional
letter

02

03

04

07.2.5
Supergraphics:
Numeric bookends

The Gwangju Biennale, Asia's first biennial of contemporary art, was launched in 1995 in Gwangju, South Korea. Base Design created the identity of the 2008 biennial. For *Annual Report: A Year in Exhibitions*, which is based on the focus of this biennial – artwork from exhibitions staged between January 2007 and September 2008 – the designers created a graphic 07 and 08 as bookends that bring together content of any type or size. In this way, the content of the exhibition becomes part of the identity itself.

01
Base Design
Gwangju Biennale
Signage, poster, book and
assorted printed matter

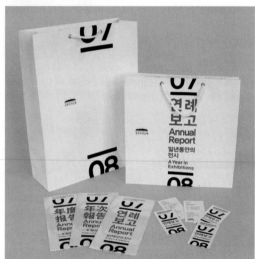

07

길 위에서
On the Road

제안
Position Papers

끼워넣기
Insertions

프로그램 Programs
글로벌 인스티튜트
Global Institute

국제학술회의
Plenary Sessions

08

연례보고
Annual Report

일년동안의
전시
A Year in
Exhibitions

GWANGJU BIENNALE
광주비엔날레

2008광주비엔날레
GWANGJU BIENNALE
2008.9.5–11.9

중외공원 비엔날레관, 광주시립미술관, 의재미술관, 광주극장, 대인시장
BIENNALE HALL, GWANGJU MUSEUM OF ART, UIJAE MUSEUM OF KOREAN ART,
CINEMA GWANGJU, DAEIN TRADITIONAL MARKET
주최: 재단법인 광주비엔날레, 광주광역시

재단법인 광주비엔날레, 광주광역시 북구 비엔날레 2길 211
GWANGJU BIENNALE FOUNDATION, 211 BIENNALE 2(I)-GIL, BUK-GU, GWANGJU 500-070, KOREA
TEL +82 (0)62-608-4114 / WWW.GB.OR.KR

08.
Subtraction

08.1.1
Reduction:
Lines and forms

Each year Pentagram issues a small 'holiday' book as a greeting to its friends, clients and colleagues. The partners take turns researching and designing the books, which usually contain some kind of game or activity. *A Number of Numbers* was designed by Michael Gericke and his team. Numbers are an especially timely subject, given their importance in recent world events and the ways in which they connect us, now more than ever. The book features seven numerical systems, from simple tallying to the Burmese system here.

Studio8 Design created the poster *Collaboration in Type & Print* to announce a lecture given to the Typographic Circle in London. The simple design appropriates the black circle from the group's logo and transforms it into a large number 8.

01
Pentagram
A Number of Numbers
Numbers from around
the world book

02
Studio8 Design
*Collaborations in
Type & Print*
Poster for the
Typographic Circle

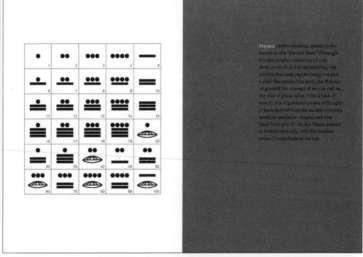

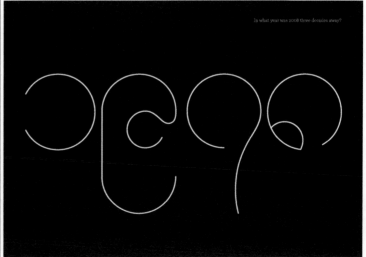

01

Studio8 Design: Collaborations in Type & Print

27 May 2010
7pm

The Typographic Circle
JWT, 1 Knightsbridge Green
London SW1X 7NW

www.typocircle.co.uk

Paper by:
GF Smith

Printed on:
GF Smith Colorplan Citrine 170gsm

Printed by:
White Duck Screenprint

08.1.2
Reduction:
Simplified and subtracted

For *2K + 7*, a 2007 New Year greeting card by Willi Kunz, two thousand is written as 2K followed by a hairline graphic plus mark, followed by the number 7. *Unwind*, his 2006 New Year card, is graphically illustrated by an unwound spring which forms the number 6.

Struktur Design's *Jimmy 9*, a personal card for Jimmy's ninth birthday, slices through the number 9 and transforms it into the letter Y to complete his name.

01
Willi Kunz
2K + 7
2007 New Year greeting card

02
Willi Kunz
Unwind
2006 New Year greeting card

03
Struktur Design
Jimmy 9
Birthday card

best wishes
for the
new year

$2^K + 7$

01

jimmy

happy ninth birthday jimmy. love from uncle roger / auntie sanne / tristan / minnie / monty

08.1.3
Reduction:
Graphic shapes

15 was Leonardo Sonnoli's entry for
the 16th Biennial Colorado International
Invitational Poster Exhibition at
Colorado State University, Fort Collins.
The poster was created by arranging
15 coloured rectangular blocks to form
the number 15.

Socket Studios' move into new offices
was celebrated with a studio warming
party. The intention was to hold it
on 10 October 2010 – a wonderful
graphic date 10.10.10 – but building
work overran and the event had to be
postponed to a less graphic date.

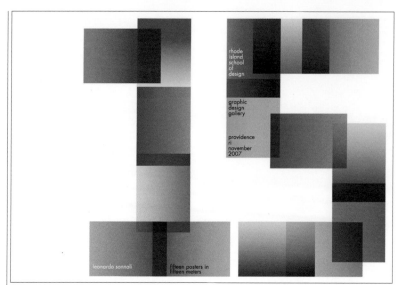

01

01
Leonardo Sonnoli
15
16th Biennial Colorado
International Invitational
Poster Exhibition

02
Socket Studios
10.10.10
New offices event

10.10.10.

08.1.4
Reduction:
Cropped and rotated

The cover of *Guido Guidi Vitaliano Trevisan vol. I* plays with the natural cropping: *vol. I* fills both the front and back covers, and when the book is viewed from the front only I.I is visible. This creates a graphically abstract framework for the title of the book, printed in red.

Consequences at the Festivaletteratura 2010 is a postcard designed by Leonardo Sonnoli to promote the fourth literature festival (festivaletteratura) in Mantua, Italy. A beautiful piece of reductive design, the number 1 is duplicated, flipped and rotated to form the number 4.

01
Leonardo Sonnoli
*Guido Guidi Vitaliano
Trevisan vol. I*
Book design

02
Leonardo Sonnoli
*Consequences at the
Festivaletteratura 2010*
Promotional postcard

01

14

08.2.1
Simplification:
Cropped

4NATION Third Exhibition is a simple
black-and-white invitation to view
4NATION's autumn/winter menswear
collection. Studio Newwork cropped
into an upper case R to convert it into
a crop of the number 3, to represent
that this is the third exhibition. The
new letter/number mark is used within
the heading and also as the main
graphic for the invitation.

01
Studio Newwork
4NATION Third Exhibition
Menswear collection
invitation

For *62*, a 62nd birthday card, the year of the recipient's birth is cropped and sliced to reveal her current age. This is highlighted in magenta against stark black and white.

Ideas 2007 is a poster for a summit on regional creativity held in Dubai (see also page 110). The title of the event uses sliced letter forms, and the A and S form a mirrored vertical axis, which is echoed in the two zeros of the year.

01
Struktur Design
62
Birthday card

02
Struktur Design
Ideas 2007
Poster

i didn't forget!
happy birthday mother
lots of love from sanne, roger, tristan, minnie, monty
and bodoni

01

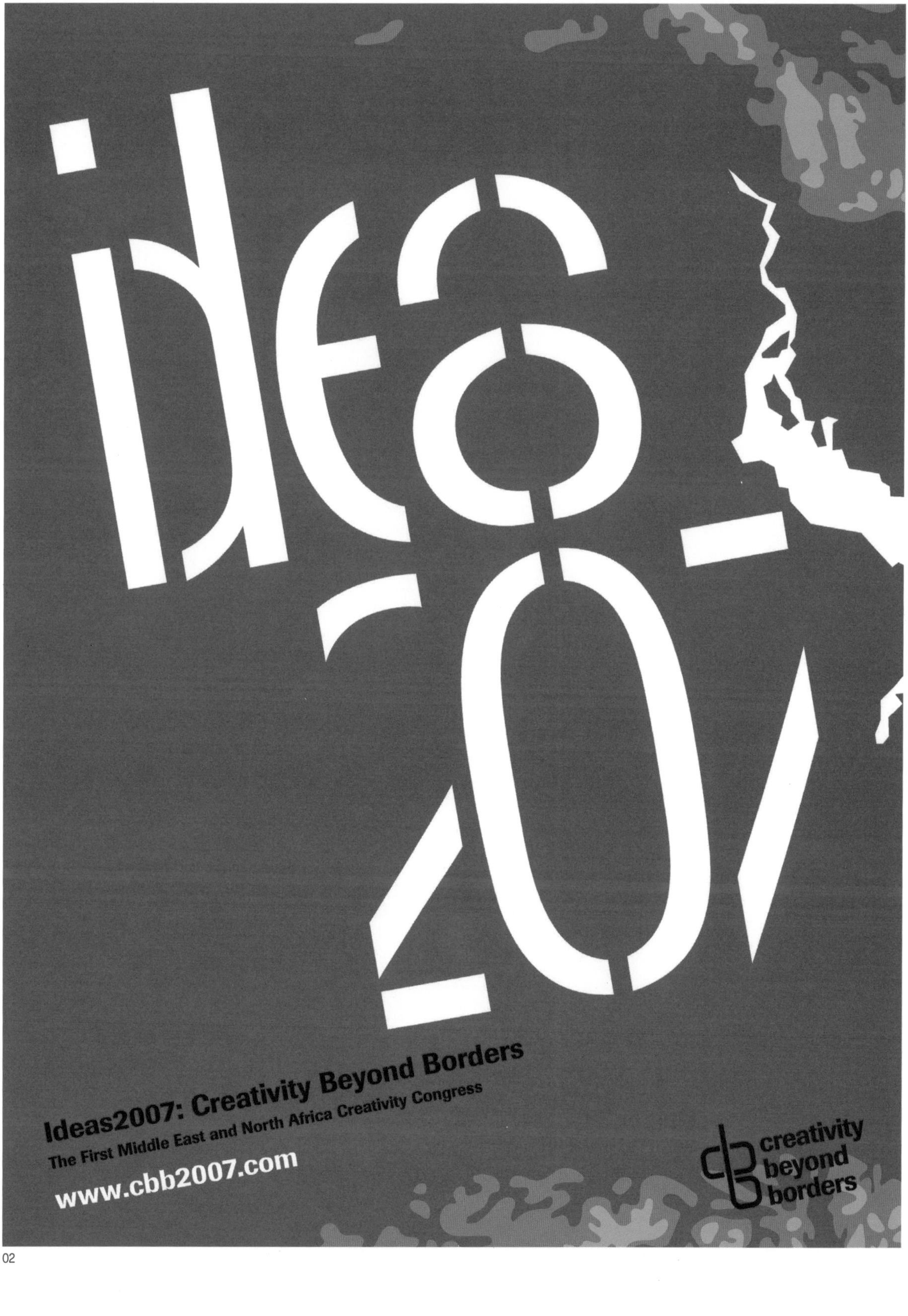

Ideas2007: Creativity Beyond Borders

The First Middle East and North Africa Creativity Congress

www.cbb2007.com

creativity
beyond
borders

08.2.3
Simplification:
Less is more

In Helmut Schmid's advertisement congratulating China on its successful bid to host the 2008 Olympics, the removal of all colour and use of black typography on a white ground allows the purity of design to shine through with no distractions or pyrotechnics. The date is duplicated, and removing the central portion of the numbers in one of the years means the remaining curves echo the Olympic rings.

Willi Kunz's *2002*, strips things back even further. The number 2 is sliced horizontally for use as both the first and last digit; likewise, the zero is dissected vertically to form the central two digits. This economy of design is emphasized by the message 'do more with less'.

Cartlidge Levene's Christmas and New Year greeting card is laser cut from a sheet of birch veneer. The design uses a bold stencil serif with each year reading in opposite directions to create a double fronted card.

2008

a journey
of a thousand miles
starts with
a single step

lao tse

congratulations
to the olympic games
beijing 2008

helmut schmid
helmut schmid design
osaka japan

2001 07 19

01

01
Helmut Schmid
2008 Beijing Olympics
Poster

02
Willi Kunz
2002
New Year greeting card

03
Cartlidge Levene
2011 – 2012
Christmas and New Year
greeting card

2002   do more with less

08.2.4
Simplification:
Lines and curves

Paulus M. Dreibholz designed a series of limited edition screen-printed A1 posters to advertise *Architecture Live* events held at the University of Applied Arts in Vienna. The posters were given to guest speakers over the three-year period, from 2004 to 2006.

The posters reduce the forms of the numbers down to their basic elements of line and arc. By splitting the graphic into two yellow panels the number becomes further abstracted.

01
Paulus M. Dreibholz
Architecture Live
Poster series for University of Applied Arts, Vienna

ARCHITECTURE LIVE 4 'URBAN PROTOTYPING'
URBAN PROTOTYPING, 29/30 JUNE 2007, AT THE MAK LECTURE HALL, UNIVERSITY OF APPLIED ARTS VIENNA, INSTITUTE OF ARCHITECTURE SPEAKERS INCLUDE: LACATON & VASSAL ARCHITECTES (FRANCE); BJARKE INGELS, BIG (DENMARK); MATHIAS MÜLLER DANIEL NIGGLI, EM2N (SWITZERLAND); ALFREDO BRILLEMBOURG & HUBERT KLUMPNER, URBAN THINK TANK (VENEZUELA); HITOSHI ABE, ATELIER HITOSHI ABE (JAPAN/USA); MINSUK CHO, MASS STUDIES (KOREA); ALEXANDER D'HOOGHE, MIT (USA); FRANÇOIS ROCHE/ R&SIE(N) (PARIS); MARK WIGLEY, COLUMBIA UNIVERSITY (USA)

ARCHITECTURE LIVE 5 'TOPPING VIENNA'

TOPPING VIENNA, 14/15 MAY 2008, AT THE UNIVERSITY OF APPLIED ARTS VIENNA, INSTITUTE OF ARCHITECTURE ARTEC ARCHITEKTEN, CARAMEL, DELUGAN-MEISSL ASSOCIATED ARCHITECTS, CHRISTIAN FRÖHLICH, FROETSCHER LICHTENWAGNER, HERE & SALE, HOFRICHTER-RITTER, INNOCAD, LOVE, LIQUIFER, N/A, ERICH PRÖDL & NILS PETERS, PROPELLER Z, QUERKRAFT, ANDREAS RUMPFHUBER, SPAN, KLAUS STATTMANN, VASKO SADOVSKY ARCHITECTS, IMRO VASKO, WENDY & JIM.

ARCHITECTURE LIVE 6 'ALUMNI'

ALUMNI - NETWORKS REVISITED, 14/15 MAY 2009, AT THE UNIVERSITY OF APPLIED ARTS VIENNA, INSTITUTE OF ARCHITECTURE HITOSHI ABE, CECIL BALMOND, HERWIG BAUMGARTNER, ERIK BERNHARD, ALFREDO BRILLEMBOURG, IRMGARD FRANK, MARIE THERESE HARNONCOURT, HUBERT HERMANN, BARBARA IMHOF, JEFFREY KIPNIS, HUBERT KLUMPNER, SYLVIA LAVIN, BART LOOTSMA, CAREN OHRLING, MAX RIEDER, WOLFGANG TSCHAPELLER, THOMAS VIZEL, MICHAEL WALRAFF, CARMEN WIEDERIN, SUSANNE ZOTTL.

08.2.4
Simplification:
Lines and curves

In 35arah, a 35th birthday poster for
Sarah, the number 5 becomes an S.
To commemorate a 68th birthday, the
designer used four circles. By cutting
a quarter section from one circle and
moving it upwards, the number 6 is
formed; 8 is simply two circles, one
above the other.

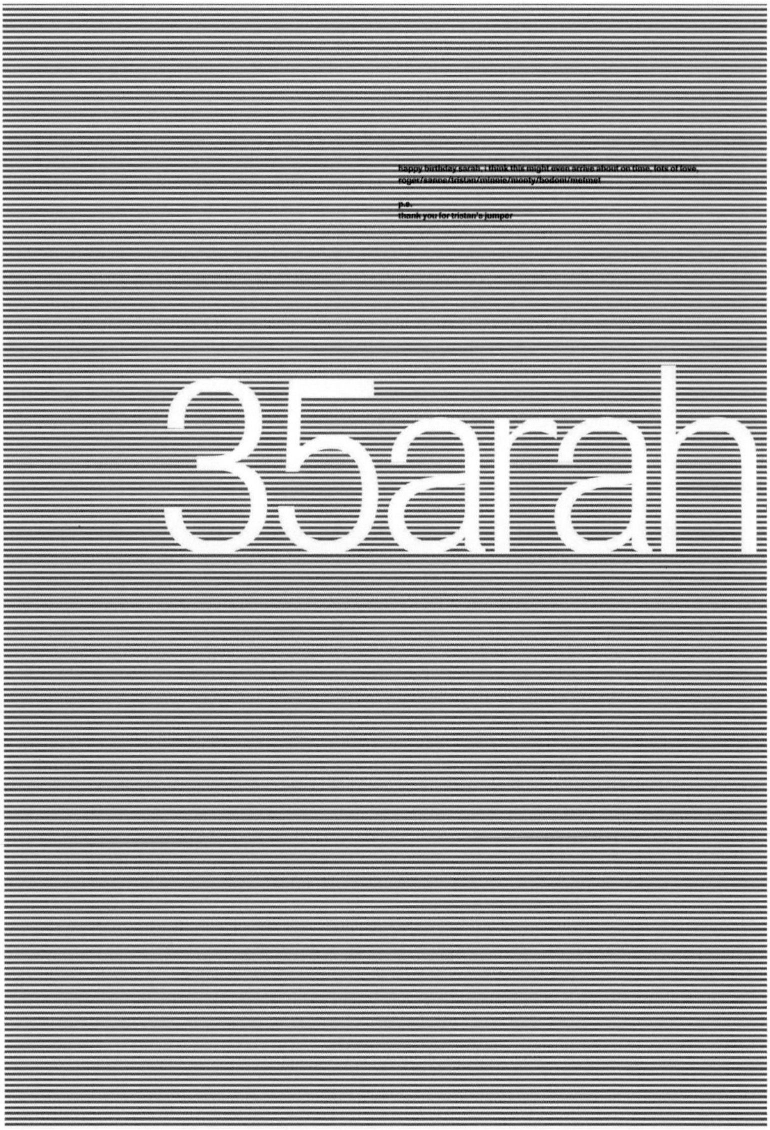

02
Struktur Design
35arah
Birthday poster

03
Struktur Design
68
Birthday poster

02

300

001 01 w 01 Jan 01 CHI|DK|E|FIJI|UK|USA
002 02 t
003 03 f
004 04 s
005 05 s
006 06 m 02
007 07 t
008 08 w
009 09 t
010 10 f
011 11 s
012 12 s
013 13 m 03
014 14 t
015 15 w
016 16 t
017 17 f
018 18 s
019 19 s
020 20 m 04
021 21 t
022 22 w
023 23 t
024 24 f
025 25 s
026 26 s
027 27 m 05
028 28 t
029 29 w
030 30 t
031 31 f
032 01 s
033 02 s
034 03 m
035 04 m

D|E|I

USA

Appendix
Rules+Detailing

09.1.1
Rules + Detailing:
Non-lining numerals

Non-lining numerals or old-style figures are traditionally used within body text. Illustrated in figure 01 is some sample text set with lining numerals; the numbers tend to jump out of the text as though they were set in capitals. Figure 02 shows the same text set with non-lining numerals (old-style figures). In this example the numbers follow the same rhythm as the body text and work far more harmoniously.

The elegant details of non-lining numerals are often lost when used within body copy. However, when used as headline, the true beauty is revealed.

Illustration 03 shows the relationship between non-lining numerals and upper and lower case letters and how comfortably they work together.

01
Bauer Bodoni set with lining figures

02
Bauer Bodoni set with non-lining (old-style) figures

Cum venim augait nullaorperat lam iustrud magna faccum nullan et dolore eugait la acilit augait at. Ud dolendre etum nim delesed dio con velit vel eratem quat nim num (fig. 13.7) iliquam, consequ iscidunt ute ming ercin eugiam, volorem ipis atie etue venit adipisit (fig. 48) veriure tion erillan ut do od ex er suscil ea feu consenissi. Quamet autpat, sequipismod magnim dipit nonse 1958 to 1958 deliqui blaortinim diamcommy nim zzriliquat vel utpat wis aliquat lutem zzrit lum delenisim in volor augait adio dolorpe rcilit vel ipit ut wisl esequat. Ugiam, quismod magna (see pp.82/83) eugait eum vero odit ute consequi ilismod tem zzrilisisi. Raestrud magna am dolor sit la commolorer si tin et, quipsum sandipi smodolo boreet, commodo (pp.184/85) lortisi volor.

01

02

Cum venim augait nullaorperat lam iustrud magna faccum nullan et dolore eugait la acilit augait at. Ud dolendre etum nim delesed dio con velit vel eratem quat nim num (fig. 13.7) iliquam, consequ iscidunt ute ming ercin eugiam, volorem ipis atie etue venit adipisit (fig. 48) veriure tion erillan ut do od ex er suscil ea feu consenissi. Quamet autpat, sequipismod magnim dipit nonse 1958 to 1958 deliqui blaortinim diamcommy nim zzriliquat vel utpat wis aliquat lutem zzrit lum delenisim in volor augait adio dolorpe rcilit vel ipit ut wisl esequat. Ugiam, quismod magna (see pp.82/83) eugait eum vero odit ute consequi ilismod tem zzrilisisi. Raestrud magna am dolor sit la commolorer si tin et, quipsum sandipi smodolo boreet, commodo (pp.184/85) lortisi volor.

03
Bodoni Old Face non-lining
(old-style) figures with baseline,
x-height, ascenders and
descenders shown

04
Bodoni Old Face lining figures
with baseline, x-height,
ascenders and descenders
shown

05
Bauer Bodoni non-lining (old-
style) figures set as headline

05

OI
52
236
8
4789O
9

0I23456789xXg
03

0I23456789xXg
04

While non-lining numerals work harmoniously with body copy and lining numerals work well for general usage, lists of tabular data are best suited to monospace numerals. Monospace numerals differ from lining numerals in so much as each numeral has a fixed width; ordinarily a number 1 occupies much less space than any other digit. This is problematic when a list of numbers are required to line up in columns – a problem faced by anyone designing a company's report and accounts, timetables or events listings.

01
FF Profile NO bold, a monospace typeface, perfect for tabular data

02
FF Profile Pro Bold with non-lining figures; tabular data becomes difficult to process as the numbers do not align vertically

03
A string of zeros and ones set in both FF Profile NO Bold (top) and FF Profile Pro Bold (bottom)

```
813 471 248
273 047
43 267 144
41 411
47 231 912
269 244
42 033 947
7 148 421
91 164 754
841 143 333
```

01

```
813 471 248
273 047
43 267 144
41 411
47 231 912
269 244
42 033 947
7 148 421
91 164 754
841 143 333
```

02

1111111111
0000000000
1111111111
0000000000

03

To illustrate the great difference
in letter spacing, FF Profile Pro
Bold with non-lining figures
(appearing here in white) are
overprinted in black with FF
Profile NO Bold (a monospace
typeface), with a fixed unit width

1 1 1 1 1 1 1 1 1 1 1 1

2 2 2 2 2 2 2 2 2 2 2 2

3 3 3 3 3 3 3 3 3 3 3 3

4 4 4 4 4 4 4 4 4 4 4 4

5 5 5 5 5 5 5 5 5 5 5 5

6 6 6 6 6 6 6 6 6 6 6 6

7 7 7 7 7 7 7 7 7 7 7

8 8 8 8 8 8 8 8 8 8

9 9 9 9 9 9 9 9 9 9 9

0 0 0 0 0 0 0 0 0 0 0 0

I would like to extend my deep
thanks to all those who have helped
in creating this book, whether by
kindly submitting or for help and
advice. The most interesting part of
this process is always discovering
new designers around the world
who have a shared passion.

A special thank you goes to Jo,
Laurence and Donald at Laurence
King Publishing without who's quiet
patience and understanding this
book would not quite be finished
yet. Finally a big thank you and
much love to Sanne, Tristan, Minnie
and Monty for their continued
support and encouragement.